Joh

The Wealthiest Man in American History

By Michael W. Simmons

Table of Contents

Introduction 4

Chapter One: The Origins of John D. Rockefeller
.... 7

Chapter Two: Young Man in a Hurry 40

Chapter Three: Rockefeller & Andrews 67

Chapter Four: Rockefeller, Andrews, and Flagler
.... 101

Chapter Five: Standard Oil 128

Chapter Six: Monopoly 159

Chapter Seven: Philanthropy 182

Further Reading 228

Introduction

"Probably in the life of every one there comes a time when he is inclined to go over again the events, great and small, which have made up the incidents of his work and pleasure, and I am tempted to become a garrulous old man, and tell some stories of men and things which have happened in an active life.

In some measure I have been associated with the most interesting people our country has produced, especially in business—men who have helped largely to build up the commerce of the United States, and who have made known its products all over the world. These incidents which come to my mind to speak of seemed vitally important to me when they happened, and they still stand out distinctly in my memory.

Just how far any one is justified in keeping what he regards as his own private affairs from the public, or in defending himself from attacks, is a mooted point. If one talks about one's experiences, there is a natural temptation to charge one with traveling the easy road to egotism; if one keeps silence, the inference of [vi]wrong-doing is sometimes even more difficult to meet, as it would then be said that there is no valid defence to be offered.

It has not been my custom to press my affairs forward into public gaze; but I have come to see that if my family and friends want some record of things which might shed light on matters that have been somewhat discussed, it is right that I should yield to their advice, and in this informal way go over again some of the events which have made life interesting to me."

John D. Rockefeller, *Random Reminiscences of Men and Events*

Chapter One: The Origins of John D. Rockefeller

The Rockefeller family

John Davison Rockefeller, the richest man in American history, was born on July 8, 1839 to William "Bill" Rockefeller and Eliza Davison Rockefeller. The Rockefeller family had migrated to America from Germany in the first decades of the eighteenth century, settling first in Pennsylvania, then in New Jersey, where they remained until 1832. That year, Bill Rockefeller's parents, Godfrey and Lucy, moved the family northwest. According to family legend, Godfrey wished to resettle in Michigan, but Lucy, a former schoolteacher who had little confidence in her alcoholic husband's judgment, refused to travel such a distance. Instead, they traveled to Richmond, a tiny town in the sparsely settled wilderness of upstate New York, where Godfrey had purchased land. The journey to New York took two years, the family walking most of the distance alongside the covered wagon that contained all of their worldly possessions. They were accompanied by all of their children, save for Bill, who was then twenty-two. No one was certain where Bill was when the family left New Jersey; at that age, he already had a habit of disappearing for long periods of time. He joined the rest of his family in Richmond in 1835, about a year after their arrival in the area.

John D. Rockefeller's father was a larger than life character with a talent for confidence schemes and hard bargains. He was clever, charming, capable of winning people's trust—talents which he used to make money and get what he wanted out of life. Bill came from a long line of farmers, but he had no interest in earning his living through a lifetime of hard, often fruitless labor. There were better ways to make more money, faster ways—so long as one didn't mind telling a few lies along the way. Over the course of his life Bill Rockefeller was a peddler, a fraud, a rapist, and eventually a bigamist. As Rockefeller biographer Ida Tarbell famously remarked, virtually the only vice the famous capitalist's father did not practice was hard drinking. Bill's father Godfrey, on the other hand, was drunk more or less constantly, and either his poor example, or the austere example of Bill's intelligent, pious mother led him to steer clear of alcohol.

Bill Rockefeller met his first wife, John's mother, Eliza Davison, when he finally joined his parents and siblings in Richmond in 1835, about a year after they had set up residence there. The manner of Bill and Eliza's first meeting, founded in trickery and deceit, was to set the tone for their entire marriage. Bill arrived in the neighborhood in the guise of a deaf and mute peddler, wearing a slate on a string around his neck which proclaimed that he could neither hear nor talk, though neither of these things was true. He presented himself in the local tavern and wrote the words "Where is the house of Godfrey Rockefeller?" on the slate, and was given directions to his father's house. Bill found it useful, pretending to be deaf, as it meant other people spoke more freely around him, often mentioning useful tidbits of information that Bill acted on to further his schemes. It was probably by eavesdropping in this manner that Bill learned of the existence of a prosperous farmer named John Davison who had a large farm some thirty miles northwest of Richmond. Bill was often in that area, because he had to spread his peddling across a large range of territory, in order to avoid reprisals from the law when his "miraculous" patent cures failed to achieve the desired results. Bill learned that Davison had a pretty young daughter, the 24-year old Eliza, and that Davison meant to settle a decent amount of money on Eliza when she married. Eventually, inevitably, Bill made his way to the Davison farm to meet John and Eliza for himself.

When Eliza Davison first set eyes on Bill, he was still pretending that he couldn't hear or speak, but he cut an impressive figure nonetheless; he was tall and strong with a full red beard and always made a point of dressing in fancy embroidered silk waistcoats. The fact that he had come seemingly from nowhere only enhanced his appeal as a romantic wanderer. Eliza was so taken in by his charming, mysterious manner that she remarked that if "that peddler" were not deaf and dumb, she would marry him. It was the sort of comment which the discreet, modest teenager would never have made in the hearing of a man who could understand what she was saying. But it was for precisely the purpose of collecting such valuable insights that Bill maintained his deaf-and-dumb ruse, and he quickly turned it to his advantage. Having established his bona fides in the neighborhood by re-connecting with his family, and playing off the deaf-and-dumb ruse as joke, Bill began to court Eliza. Her father John was instantly suspicious of this suddenly smooth-talking huckster and foresaw that Eliza would know a great deal of misery if she married him. But at 24 she was old enough to marry whomever she wished without her parents' permission, and it was not long before Bill had won her over. They were married, not in Eliza's father's house, but in a friend's home—John Davison could not bear to attend the ceremony.

Bill Rockefeller had built a home for himself and his new bride just half a mile from his parents' house, but at an inconvenient distance from any other neighbors. The Rockefellers were therefore the only people Eliza had to socialize with during the first few years of her marriage, as Bill tended to vanish mysteriously for long periods of time, never leaving behind a word as to where he was going. It was hard for Eliza to feel at home with the hard-drinking Godfrey, the bombastic, unreliable Bill, and the other boisterous

Rockefeller relations, who were all crammed together into one small house. During family gatherings and celebrations Eliza often excused herself from the crowd and went to sit alone in an empty room. Only in her mother-in-law, Lucy, did Eliza find a likeminded companion, another intelligent, deeply principled and religious woman who had made an unfortunate mistake in her choice of husband and now had to live with the consequences.

There was one other person living in the Richmond house where John Rockefeller and his older sister were to be born: a girl named Nancy Brown whom Bill had supposedly hired to help Eliza with the housework. To Eliza's distress, she quickly discovered that Bill had brought Nancy there because she was his mistress. Around the same time that Eliza's first child was born, a daughter who was named Lucy for her grandmother, Nancy Brown also gave birth to a baby girl who had been fathered by Bill.

Remarkably, Eliza bore no ill will towards the servant girl, but treated her with compassion. When John was born about a year later, Nancy Brown also gave birth to a second child, another daughter. The presence of Brown and her illegitimate children under the same roof as Eliza and her two children would have been taken as an insult by virtually anyone else, but Eliza seemed to feel that Nancy had been placed in an impossible position by her husband, a man in whose character she had been unhappily deceived, and she continued to treat the small family living under her roof kindly.

Eventually, John Davison caught wind of the fact that Bill Rockefeller was sleeping with Nancy Brown and housing their illegitimate children under the same roof as John's daughter and grandchildren. At his insistence, Bill moved Nancy and her daughters to a small house of their own, after which he more or less abandoned them, save for the occasional present of clothing or supplies dropped on their doorstep. At least one of the girls grew up to be a respected schoolteacher, and it is uncertain whether she ever knew that she was the half-sister of the richest man in the world, or whether John himself knew that he had half-sisters living in the town where he had been born. Because Bill and Eliza moved away from Richmond when John was only three, his memories of that period of his life were always indistinct; he could remember climbing the hill to his grandparents' house, where his grandmother kept a "physic bush", a small tree whose leaves and roots Lucy Rockefeller believed to have medicinal qualities.

Bill Rockefeller was, in short, one of those legendary figures of the early 19th century American frontier, a snake oil salesman, a man who travels from town to town and peddles "medicines" that were supposed to cure everything from stomach upset to cancer, and some of the remedies he concocted for sale were brewed from Lucy's physic bush. It is certain that his mother believed they possessed healing properties; perhaps Bill believed so as well, though he also sold medicines that were little more than alcohol stewed with bitter herbs—or sometimes, even less wholesome ingredients.

Moravia

Peddling these cures and remedies from town to town took Bill Rockefeller away from his family for long periods of time—he would vanish one morning, having given his wife no notice of when he was likely to return again, and reappear weeks or months later, always flush with cash. Sometimes, it seemed that Bill had a great deal of money; he was known to keep buckets of coins and boxes of rolled up bills in his bedroom. He was always well dressed, to the point of being gaudy. Other times, he was entirely penniless, and took out large loans to cover his debts. While he was away from his family, he instructed the local merchants to give Eliza whatever she asked for, with the promise that he would settle up in full as soon as he returned to the area. It seems that he always made good on his promises, but the arrangement gave Eliza great anxiety nonetheless. She never knew how long Bill would be away, and the longer he was gone, the more things she had to buy on credit—credit that might be cut off at any moment, at the whim of the shopkeepers. She learned how to be extremely frugal, and she practiced strict bookkeeping, so that no penny was wasted.

When John was three, Bill moved his family to Moravia, where he built them a modest but attractive house with a view of the lake. In Moravia, they were reasonably close to Eliza's father, which made her feel less anxious during Bill's protracted absences. Shortly after the family moved to Moravia, Eliza gave birth to twins, a boy named Frank and a girl named

Frances. Most of John Rockefeller's earliest memories of childhood begin in Moravia; when he was an old man he spoke with great fondness of the house with the beautiful view of the lake and the trees through the windows. His sister Frances was sickly from her birth, and she died when she was two years old. John was thought to be too sensitive to know the truth, so he was sent to a field to gather stones while Frances was buried. Throughout his life he had a horror of death; his mother must have sensed it even then, and wished to protect him from the sight of his sister being lowered into the ground.

Because Bill was away for so much of John Rockefeller's childhood, his character was shaped primarily by his mother, who was loving but strict, a woman of neat, orderly habits with a disciplinarian streak. As John was her oldest son, she came to rely on him to supply his father's place when he was still very young. He carried an adult's responsibility at an age when most children were free to play and run around. Religion played a large role in the life of the family; Eliza negotiated with a neighbor, who attended the local Methodist church, to take her and the children part of the way to the Baptist church they attended faithfully every Sunday. Rockefeller remained a devout Christian throughout his life, partly because he discovered as a young child that though many members of his family were unreliable—namely his Rockefeller relations—the churches he attended provided a community that was like a family. The Christian faith also provided moral guidance for believers, helping them avoid the kind of pitfalls that could ruin a person's character, such as alcohol addiction. It also provided a means to combat the evils of the world, such as slavery. John Rockefeller passed his childhood and youth in the years leading up to the Civil War, the era which gave birth to the religious activism movement. During John's youth, the Southern Baptist church split with the Northern Baptist church over the issue of slavery; Northern

Baptists were staunch abolitionists, where Southern Baptists believed that slavery was an institution ordained by God. As a boy, John was deeply affected by the conviction that he was called, as a Christian, to effect positive change in the world using whatever talents and resources he possessed.

Curiously, considering what he achieved later in life, John was not considered to be especially talented when he was a boy. He was a plodder, a faithful hard worker—slow, but dogged. He demonstrated no flashes of brilliance or genius as a student. He had an indisputable talent for mathematics, however. Numbers seemed to fascinate him. Since he was a child, he had helped his mother keep their household accounts, and in the orderly columns of figures he found an almost transcendental meaning that most people find in poetry or music. Despite the fact that every penny of the family's finances had to be closely watched, Eliza insisted that her children put pennies in the offering plate every Sunday, which seems to have formed an indelible connection between money and religion in Rockefeller's mind—not the use of religion to make money, a scheme which probably would have appealed to his father, but a concept of stewardship, the idea that God placed money in the hands of those who would turn around and give it right back, to do good in the world. Ron Chernow writes of how this attitude, inculcated in Rockefeller from boyhood, came to influence his charitable giving after Rockefeller made his fortune:

"As to why God had singled out John D. Rockefeller for such spectacular bounty, Rockefeller always adverted to his own adherence to the doctrine of stewardship—the notion of the wealthy man as a mere instrument of God, a temporary trustee of his money, who devoted it to good causes. 'It has seemed as if I was favored and got increase because the Lord knew that I was going to turn around and give it back.'"

John Rockefeller was to become not only the richest man in history but the most generous philanthropist in America, pioneering the practice of establishing charitable foundations that targeted specific causes and endowing them with rich incomes. He believed throughout his life that God had enabled him to acquire massive wealth precisely so he could use that money to do God's work in the world. For this reason, he was understandably offended when he later developed a reputation as a robber baron and a selfish tyrant in the business world.

Just as the young John Rockefeller was considered to be an unpromising student, he was also regarded as an unremarkable individual—a pleasant, reliable, somber boy who seemed to blend into the background, no matter where he went. Adults who had known Rockefeller as a child were astonished by his rapid rise to fame and fortune, often remarking that he was entirely forgettable as a boy, that there was nothing in him which inspired curiosity as to what he would accomplish when he was grown up. His younger brother William was considered far more popular and likable than John, mostly because William had the open, engaging, talkative manners of their father, if not his propensity for deceit and cunning. John, by contrast, having been forced to assume adult responsibilities at a young age, was so reserved, so controlled, so lacking in childish humor and impulsiveness, that people looked right past him. Only his mother seemed to realize that John's preternatural self-control—which was a remarkable talent in itself, albeit one that, by its very nature, called no attention to itself—masked a deep sensitivity. He rarely demonstrated strong emotion, even as a man, but this was a skill he learned as a direct response to his father's flamboyant character and correspondingly dubious morality. If John, as a child, confided in no one, spoke little, and masked his emotions, it was probably because he had secrets to keep— secrets about his father that would bring shame on his mother and his family if they were spoken of openly. Bill's peripatetic habits and confidence schemes inspired gossip; it was regularly whispered that he was a horse thief, one of the most serious crimes a person could be accused of on the American frontier. Eliza's rigid morality, impeccable respectability, and regular habits counterbalanced Bill's unpredictability and protected her family from becoming an object of ridicule or pity. As his mother's helper, John adopted her manners. As one Rockefeller biographer puts it:

"In the towns of John's boyhood, Bill was an engaging but notorious character who prompted interminable speculation about his travels and sources of income. A boy with such a father needed to screen out malicious gossip and cultivate a brazen indifference to community opinion. This bred in him a reflexive habit of secrecy, a deep contempt for idle chatter and loose tongues that lasted a lifetime. He learned to cultivate a secretive style and a defiant attitude toward strangers."

The need for such secrecy and indifference to community opinion became all the more pressing when Bill's actions threatened to destroy the peaceful, pleasant life the family had made for itself in Moravia. For a time, Bill had seemed prepared to settle down into a more regular lifestyle, operating a timber and logging business that kept him closer to home and even made him into something like a pillar of the community. The logging business was so profitable that Bill had built a school in Moravia, painstakingly measuring out the distance so that the structure would stand at the exact center of town. But gradually, the business made less and less money, and Bill returned to wandering the surrounding territories, peddling medicines and baubles. During one of these trips, he encountered a young woman who later brought a charge of rape against him. This was a serious matter; it was extremely difficult for a woman to bring rape charges against a man in the early 19th century, and the fact that she was willing to face the public humiliation that such a legal ordeal would entail speaks to the seriousness of the offense. There are no records of a trial taking place, but the Rockefellers moved from Moravia to the town of Owego shortly afterwards, which probably indicates that he was confronted by the town authorities and told to leave the county, a common method of dealing with rape cases at the time. The failure of his business and the scandal of the rape charge permanently soured Bill Rockefeller's relationship with his father in law, John Davison. At Bill's request, Davison had loaned him two thousand dollars; when it was clear that he would have to flee the area, Davison sued Bill publicly to prevent him from skipping town without making payment. Eliza thus had to suffer the bitter humiliation of seeing her father bring suit against her own husband in a court of law.

John was not told about the rape charge, which is scarcely surprising, given his age. As an old man, however, he denied that such charges had ever been brought. They had been brought to light by Ida Tarbell, whose *History of the Standard Oil Company* had roused a massive public outcry against Rockefeller, and he naturally disdained her credibility as a journalist. Rockefeller insisted that he would have known if the move to Owego had taken place "under compulsion", despite the fact that he was only eleven years old at the time. Probably he assumed that, since his mother was in the habit of treating him like an adult and asking him to share her burdens in looking after the family, she would have shared this burden with him as well. From an outside perspective, however, it seems more likely that his mother felt that she'd placed quite enough worry and care on her son's shoulders already, without adding his father's disgrace to the rest of it.

Whatever the circumstances that prompted it, the move to Owego, which took place in 1850, came as a welcome change for the whole family. Granted, the house in Moravia was very pleasantly situated, and Eliza and the children had enjoyed living so close to John Davison. But once they were settled in Owego, Bill's absences became even more prolonged than they had been before, and this seems to have provided Eliza and John with some relief. The family was, in the words of one biographer, "stronger without Bill". Granted, John Rockefeller had great affection for his father when he was small. Bill would return from his long trips like Santa Claus, his saddlebags heavy with gold and presents for the children. His embroidered waistcoats and loud laughter and raucous stories made him the instant center of attention, a brief but entertaining reprieve from the stolidity of Eliza Davison Rockefeller's orderly household. But after his legal troubles in Moravia, Bill abandoned all pretense of being a respectable member of the community or a reliable presence in his children's lives, and by then John was finally old enough to see through his father's glittering façade to the unstable, unprincipled character underneath. Bill had ceased to be a figure of mystery and fascination and began to be simply disappointing. Rockefeller always defended his father's reputation, particularly when journalists began to dig into his family's past, but as he grew older, he simply preferred not to speak of Bill. He felt that he had a religious duty not to hold grudges, against anyone—not his business rivals, not Ida Tarbell, and certainly not members of his own family. But on the very rare occasions he ever betrayed a flash of anger when speaking with an interviewer about his past, it was usually because they had mentioned something about his father's checkered past.

In comparison to Moravia, which was a large village, Owego was a proper town, with fine houses in the downtown district, shops, churches, and paved streets. Railroads transported people to Owego from all over the country, and from all over the world—the young John was deeply impressed when he spotted "a real, live Frenchman" at the train station one day. Growing up in isolated, rural areas made Owego seem exciting and cosmopolitan by comparison, the kind of place where a poor, uncultured boy could rub shoulders with boys his own age from wealthier families with a more sophisticated experience of the world. During the three years the family lived in Owego, John and his brother William had the opportunity to attend Owego Academy, which was the best school in that part of the country at that time. Their fellow scholars were from much wealthier families. A family friend had to pay for John and William's schoolbooks, and when a photographer took a school portrait, the Rockefeller boys weren't allowed to appear in the picture, because their suits were so shabby that it was thought they would be an embarrassment to the parents of the other children. But John, at least, never seemed to mind being treated differently for being poor. He was already possessed of a sober adult's single mindedness and steadiness of purpose. At Owego Academy, he learned many of the skills that would serve him when he began his career. He wrote essays every two weeks and gave speeches before his classmates, lessons which helped him to write clear and purposeful business correspondence and speak with strangers in a forthright and confident manner.

John did not make close friends at Owego Academy, but nor was he unpopular. He occasionally revealed a dry sense of humor, which came as a surprise to those who did not know him well. Whenever he expressed emotions, he did so in a controlled manner that somehow betrayed a greater depth of feeling than if he had ranted and raved. In the afternoons, when John and William returned from school, their mother sent them to a neighbor's house, where a teenage girl named Susan La Monte supervised their homework while Eliza looked after the younger children at home. After Rockefeller became famous, La Monte was one of those who recalled that John never seemed to be an especially talented student, nor did he seem to have strong feelings towards her or any member of her family, though he was always polite. Yet when one of her younger sisters died, John came to the La Monte house and lay down in the grass outside for an entire day, never speaking a word. This peculiar mourning ritual made a deep impression on Susan La Monte, hinting as it did at the strong feelings that must have run beneath the young boy's placid exterior. As Rockefeller matured, he would channel his strongest emotions into the practice of his faith, and continue to present a bland exterior to all but those who knew him best.

Ohio

In 1853, the lives of Eliza Rockefeller and her children were again uprooted when Bill moved them to a small town in Ohio about twelve miles from Cleveland, called Strongsville. The motivation for this move was mysterious to Eliza, as were almost all of Bill's actions. John, however, eventually learned the truth, and for the rest of his mother's life he would go to great lengths to shield her from ever finding it out.

While his family was enjoying a peaceful life in Owego, Bill Rockefeller had established two distinct alternate identities for himself. The first identity was that of a Dr. William A. Rockefeller, Cancer Specialist, who peddled a medicine, composed of unknown ingredients, which boldly claimed to cure all cancers—save for the very worst cases. Under his other identity, that of Dr. William Levingston, he traveled to Niagara, Ontario, in Canada, where he met and married a pretty young teenager named Margaret Allen, whose family was so charmed by this flashy huckster in his forties that they gave their support to the match. From that point onwards, Bill Rockefeller was leading a true double life. He had moved his first wife and their children to Ohio for no good reason except that it simplified the logistics of having to provide for two families at once. Eliza had always had a home of her own, in Richmond, Moravia, and in Owego, but in Strongsville she was, for a time, forced to board with her children in the home of Sarah Ann and William Humiston, Bill's sister and brother in law. The Humistons respected Eliza greatly, but living conditions were cramped, and Eliza was greatly relieved when Bill moved them to a small farm outside of Strongsville shortly afterwards. Unbeknownst to her, this was the beginning of

Bill's attempts to settle Eliza and the children in a permanent and fairly secure situation so that he could wash his hands of them with a clean conscience and spend the majority of his time with his new family in Canada.

It was Bill's design that John, who had been acting as the man of the house in his father's place for many years already, should soon assume that duty permanently. With John to look after his mother and younger siblings, it would be all the easier for Bill to live in Canada for most of the year. It seems strange, perhaps, that a man who would not scruple to take a second wife under false pretenses would trouble himself to see that his first family was looked after, but Bill had a complicated and inconsistent sense of morality. Shortly after he moved Eliza and the children to the farm, he announced that John and William should begin attending a high school in Cleveland. High school was considered optional in an age when many children attended school only until the eighth grade, if they attended school at all. But John, though he was not considered a brilliant student, wanted to attend college when he was older, so he was happy to continue his education.

John was fifteen when he began attending Central High School in Cleveland—a little older than the other boys in his year, because the school believed that his education had been patchy due to how often his family moved from town to town, and thus required him to spend an additional year in grammar school before admitting him. Despite this, he was once again lucky in his education; the high school in Cleveland had an excellent reputation. John acquitted himself as a student respectably, not shining in any particular subject, but doing well enough to get along, making enough friends to not seem an outcast. While he was living in Cleveland, he approached Dr. White, the principal of the school, and asked him for assistance in finding lodgings for his mother and younger siblings, who wished to live nearby while John and William were in the city. Dr. White responded by opening his own home to the Rockefeller family. Tellingly, when John described his mother to Dr. White, he lied and said that she was a widow. His reasons for doing so are not entirely clear, although it does suggest that Bill was already as good as in the ground as far as his son was concerned. Possibly John was trying to shield Eliza from the shame of having been more or less abandoned by her wandering husband; possibly he thought that a widow with young children would have an easier time finding respectable lodgings than a woman whose chaotic, unpredictable husband might appear at any moment without warning. It is also possible that he was also trying to screen his father's reputation, playing the role of a dutiful son to a man who scarcely deserved this honor. In any case, Eliza was to live as a widow for the rest of her life. After John made his fortune, he bought a ranch for his father and gave him huge sums of money when Bill asked for them, and the only request he ever made of his father in return was that he put aside Margaret Allen and return home to Eliza. Bill happily took his son's money, and after Eliza's death he occasionally made the trip out east to visit his grandchildren, but he refused to abandon his wife in Canada. John kept a tight lid on his anger, but whenever Bill asked him for money, John made a point of writing the checks out to William Avery Rockefeller, not to "William Levingston". John regarded it as his duty to provide for his father while he was alive, but when he died, John was determined that Margaret Allen and her family would have no legal claim to inherit any of the Rockefeller fortune.

Bill's bigamous second marriage scuttled John's plans to attend college. It was by no means a given that a boy from a working class family would go to college in those days, and many people saw higher education as a pointless indulgence—Bill was probably one of them, although his primary motivation was to leave John no choice but to get a job as soon as possible so that he could take over the responsibility of supporting his mother and younger siblings. John accepted the news that he would not be going to college with the same quiet fortitude that came to his aid in all his dealings with his father. Far from being annoyed at having to get a job at the age of sixteen, he promptly dropped out of high school, mere weeks before commencement. After taking a few business classes E.G. Folsom's Commercial College, John embarked on a job search, promoting his skills as a bookkeeper. Relentlessly treading the sidewalks of Cleveland until he found a firm that was willing to hire a boy to do a man's job, John Rockefeller embarked on the career path that would make him a rich man within the decade, and the wealthiest man in the world shortly afterward.

Chapter Two: Young Man in a Hurry

Hewitt and Tuttle

It took John two months to find employment in Cleveland after he left high school, but it was not for lack of trying. Day after day, he would get up in the morning, dress in a respectable suit, and go down the list of businesses in Cleveland that he judged likely to have need of a clerk who had experience with bookkeeping. For any young person struggling to find a first job immediately after leaving school, the process can be demoralizing, but John was not discouraged when one business after another turned him down. Truthfully, to all outward appearances, he had nothing but dogged determination and preternatural self-confidence to recommend him; no one would guess by looking at him that he had a brilliant mind for numbers.

So long as John was unemployed, he treated his job search as if it were a job in itself. Every day, he consulted his list of businesses; every day, he presented himself at one office after another, explaining the skills he possessed, and asking if there was a place for him. He was turned down by every single business on the list, but when he'd been rejected by the last one, he simply started over again. By the time he returned to the business that had rejected him the first time, a month or so would have passed, justifying a fresh inquiry. Rockefeller was inclined to wax nostalgic over this job search in his later years, idealizing the period of his youth in which everything was uncertain, and the future seemed filled with endless possibilities. "I went to the railroads, the banks, the wholesale merchants," he said "I did not go to any small establishments. I did not guess what [the job] would be, but I was after something big." Even as a sixteen-year old high school drop out with no job experience,

John had a preternatural sense of his own abilities and talents. Suggestions that he try for the kinds of jobs that teenage boys usually got, as a shop assistant or the like, were met with firm shakes of the head. He knew he was destined to make a name for himself in business; time spent working in any other field would be time wasted.

Eventually, John found a position at the firm of Hewitt and Tuttle, "commission merchants and produce shippers". As luck would have it, the firm had recently lost a bookkeeper and was in dire need of John's skills, though he was taken on in a probationary capacity at first. After his first interview, he was hired chiefly for the neatness of his penmanship—a very necessary skill in a bookkeeper in the days before Excel spreadsheets. John was ecstatic to be given a chance to prove himself, and he often reflected that the day he was hired was among the happiest days of his life. Nonetheless, he received no pay until he had been working for

Hewitt and Tuttle for three months. John took this in his stride—boys of his age were often taken on as unpaid apprentices until they had proven their mettle, and he was confident that he would quickly show his value to the company.

Any person in need of a job is bound to feel happiness and relief when the job is finally obtained, but for John Rockefeller, the work itself was also a source of great pleasure and happiness. He was in his element, sitting on a high stool, pouring over ledgers full of figures arrayed in neat columns. Anyone else probably would have found the work dry and boring, but not John Rockefeller, who had been keeping the books of his mother's household since he was a boy and had long ago come to see the practice of financial bookkeeping as a kind of bulwark against the uncertainty and chaos of the world. It is often the case that a person who truly loves their work quickly proves capable of doing that work better and more ably than coworkers people who have been doing it for longer; so it was with John. He was a better bookkeeper than either of the firm's senior partners, and if they did not realize it immediately, John did.

Rockefeller, from his earliest years, "betrayed a special affinity for accounting. He had an almost mystical faith in numbers...ledgers were sacred books that guided decisions and saved one from fallible emotion. They gauged performance, exposed fraud, and ferreted out hidden inefficiencies. In an imprecise world, they rooted things in a solid empirical reality." Ron Chernow writes that Rockefeller "chided slipshod rivals", claiming that "Many of the brightest [businessmen] kept their books in such a way that they did not actually know when they were making money on a certain operation and when they were losing." One is reminded of another founder of a great dynasty of wealthy capitalists, Mayer Rothschild, who wrote letters containing similar sentiments to his son Nathan, founder of the English branch of the Rothschild bank. Mayer Rothschild, recognizing that Nathan had terrible penmanship and no great talent for bookkeeping himself, urged him to engage a capable clerk, using language so similar to Rockefeller's that one must assume that the instinct for tidy bookkeeping inevitably accompanies financial genius.

John received no pay for his work at Hewitt and Tuttle until he had been working for them for three months. Nonetheless, he performed his duties with as much zeal as if he were their most highly respected employee. It was up to John to pay the firm's bills and collect payments owed to them. Every bill that passed through his hands was examined with minute mathematical scrutiny, and errors of only a few cents were corrected with the same exactness as if they had represented much larger figures. Often, his employers would hand a bill over to a clerk and instruct him to see the bill paid without reviewing the figures for themselves. Other clerks simply accepted the charge and remitted payment without asking further questions; Rockefeller, by contrast, went over every charge listed on the bill, did the arithmetic himself, and often came up with a different figure than the original bill had presented. Whether the sum to be paid was great or lesser than the sum named was of no consequence to him. Only exactness mattered. Once the bills had been reviewed, it was up to Rockefeller to collect payment, a notoriously thankless job—no one likes a bill collector. But Rockefeller, with his combined talents of patience, politeness, and a refusal to be put off, collected the sums owed to the company with dogged persistence, even if it meant sitting outside the doors of the debtors' business for hours at a time, until at last, unnerved, they capitulated and handed the money over. To Rockefeller, this was more than a tiresome duty; it was absolutely essential to the smooth running of the company for which he was now partly responsible. He later confessed to having anxiety dreams about those days in which he served as a bill collector.

"How many times have I dreamed now and then up to recent years that I was trying to collect those bills," he would explain, as an old man. "I would wake up exclaiming, 'I can't collect So-and So's account!" In truth, even when he was a mere clerk, Rockefeller assumed a greater degree of responsibility for the smooth running of Hewitt and Tuttle's business than the partners assumed themselves. When at last Rockefeller began to be paid for his work, he received fifty dollars for the three months of his apprenticeship, with the promise of a raise in pay that would earn him three hundred over the course of the following year. This was precisely what he had wanted most—financial independence from a mercurial father, whose letters often threatened to send him back to the family farm in Strongsville if he could not make his own way in the city. Yet he felt troubled by the pleasure he took in having his salary so elevated. "I felt like a criminal," he confessed later. As a Christian, he was on his guard against greed—but as a brilliant financial mind, he could not help being fascinated by money and all that it represented.

Erie Street Mission Baptist Church

When it came to money, specifically John Rockefeller's ambition to become a wealthy man—for that was his goal, almost from the moment he entered the world of commerce—he was conflicted, and the source of his conflicted feelings lay in his religious convictions. The love of money for its own sake, was a sin. And yet he had been thrilled, almost obsessed by money since he was a young boy, when his father Bill would return home from his mysterious wanderings carting buckets of cash with him. Granted, Bill's money never stayed in one place for long—he could pass for a wealthy man one moment and be seeking large loans from his neighbors the next. But the pursuit of gold inspired Bill's mysterious wanderings, and whenever he returned to the family home, he was laden with cash. To Bill's young son, this dramatic display made him look upon money as something more than a symbol for purchasing power. It was an almost magical thing in itself. Rockefeller knew from a young age that he possessed talents which would enable him to make large amounts of money, but he was torn between the desire to possess wealth and the concern that this desire would lead to worldly, unchristian avarice.

His anchor in these times of doubt was his membership in the Erie Street Mission Baptist Church. The Baptist denomination is perhaps one of the most uniquely American sects to be born out of the fires of the Second Great Awakening, the religious movement that spread fundamentalist Christianity through the northeast and points further west during the early 19th century. In contrast to most major sects of Christianity, the tenets of Baptist faith hold that each individual congregation is sovereign, not accountable to bishops or a diocese or any other governing body. When John Rockefeller was a boy, Baptist ministers were usually laymen, not seminary-trained theologians, and congregations were empowered to choose their own leaders without their being subject to the approval of any higher authority. Baptists enjoyed their independence, but the flip side of that independence was a lack of financial support from a larger church structure. A Catholic church, for instance, is funded (in simplistic terms) by the Vatican; Baptist churches are funded by donations, or tithes, from their members, meaning that the wealthier the congregations, the larger the church building is likely to be, and the more money it has at its disposal to look after its poorest members and fund into other charitable causes.

Erie Street Mission Baptist Church, of which Rockefeller was a staunch member for years, was called a mission church because it had been founded and funded by a far wealthier Baptist church in Cleveland. The Erie Street congregation was a close-knit unit, a substitute family that meant a great deal to a man like Rockefeller, whose own family had always looked to him for support but rarely gave it in return. Rockefeller's tireless devotion to work (not to mention the strict principles which forbade him to drink alcohol or socialize with women of "loose morals") left him little time for a social life. Church gatherings therefore provided his only social outlet. At church picnics, he drank lemonade and made friends, and admired the pretty young women without risking lewdness or immoral behavior. During church services, he found a venue for emotional release that was not available to him in his weekday life. For all of these reasons, Rockefeller was utterly devoted to the Erie Street church, and it absorbed practically all of his free time. After he was famous, one of the women of his former congregation remembered all that he had done in its service:

"In those years...Rockefeller might have been found there any Sunday sweeping out the halls, building a fire, lighting the lamps, cleaning the walks, ushering the people to their seats, studying the bible, praying, singing, performing all the duties of an unselfish and thorough going church member... He was nothing but a clerk, and had little money, and yet he gave something to every organization in the little, old church. He was always very precise about it. If he said that he would give fifteen cents, not a living soul could move him to give a penny more or a penny less... He studied his Bible regularly and diligently, and he knew what was in it."

The man who would go on to become one of the greatest philanthropists of the 19th and early 20th centuries was already, on a meager salary of three to five hundred dollars a year, pouring a significant percentage of his income into charitable giving. Not only did he tithe the customary ten percent to his church; he also set aside a few cents or a few dollars at a time for the relief of the poor, widows, men down on their luck, any member of the church who was in need. We know this, because Rockefeller kept ledgers of his personal finances from this period that were even more lovingly exact than the ledgers he kept for his employers at Hewitt and Tuttle. Rockefeller's financial acumen would also serve to save his church from being shut down when its mortgage was foreclosed upon. One of the deacons of the larger parent church which had founded the Erie Street Mission held its mortgage; one day, with very little warning, he called the note in, which was as good as a death warrant to a poor congregation. Unless the church's members could raise the two thousand dollars needed to pay off the mortgage within two weeks, it would have no choice but to close its doors. The congregation was grief-stricken—most of the people who attended the church were poor, and no single member could scrape that amount of money together, two thousand dollars being a massive sum in those days. Rockefeller, however, immediately sprang into action. After the minister made his announcement and services had concluded, Rockefeller stationed himself at the door of the church and spoke to every member individually, asking each person to pledge whatever they could reasonably spare, be it fifty dollars or fifty cents. He wrote each person's name and the amount they had pledged in a ledger—and then, with the same patient, polite persistence he used to collect payments for Hewitt and Tuttle, he rounded up every penny of the two thousand dollars before the deadline, and the Erie Street Mission Baptist Church was saved. From that point forward, John was considered the second most significant member of the church after the minister himself.

John's devotion to his faith and his church had nothing to do with his desire to become a wealthy man and succeed in the world of business, but they helped anyway. He was a young man, a relative newcomer to the city, but his involvement in the church meant that there were any number of people willing and able to vouch for his honesty, his self-discipline, and his sense of responsibility. In those days, before background checks and credit checks, the amount of credit available to a person from the local banks depended strongly on their character and reputation. When John entered the phase of his career that required him to raise large amounts of capital, he found it fairly easy to get loans, because he was so highly regarded in his church.

John Rockefeller eventually chose to leave Hewitt and Tuttle, after disagreeing with one of the partners about the amount of his annual raise. Rockefeller felt no bitterness about leaving the firm. One biographer quotes a novel by Theodore Dreiser in describing how Rockefeller felt about working for his first employers: "He could see their weaknesses and their shortcomings as a much older man might have viewed a boy's." John had been delighted to get a job at Hewitt and Tuttle, but he had never intended to stay there permanently. He knew the value of the work he was performing for the firm, and once he began to feel that he was being underpaid, he wasted no time in striking out on his own.

Clark and Rockefeller

In 1857, Henry Tuttle, the junior partner at Hewitt and Tuttle, left the firm, and John was promptly tasked with taking over all of Tuttle's duties. This, effectively, made him the company's chief bookkeeper, but where Tuttle had been paid two thousand a year for his work, John's salary was only to be five hundred a year, with the promise of a raise to six hundred the year following. The injustice of this stung John deeply—after all, the firm was only keeping afloat because of his industrious labor. But even though thoughts of leaving the firm had come into his head some time ago, he decided to remain where he was for the time being. The year of 1857 was marked by a financial slump due to interruptions in international trade caused by the Crimean War; it was, therefore, not an auspicious time for a young man to become an entrepreneur. Soon, however, the depression was over, and John was examining Hewitt's books only to discover that the firm was nearly bankrupt. At the end of 1857 John asked Hewitt to raise his salary to eight hundred a year; when Hewitt refused, John resigned, and accepted an offer to go into business with a former classmate, Maurice Clark.

Clark's offer of a partnership depended on John's being able to raise two thousand dollars' worth of investment capital, money he did not have. He *had* managed, over the course of only three years, to save eight hundred dollars, the equivalent of more than a year's salary, but it wasn't enough. Rescue came from an unexpected source: Bill Rockefeller. John's father told him that he would be willing to loan John the other twelve hundred dollars he needed—but he would be charging ten per cent interest on that loan. This was a higher rate than John would have paid on a loan from a bank, but there was no reason for a bank to give such a substantial loan to a young man of twenty, so John accepted his father's offer. Lest this seem like a charitable act on Bill Rockefeller's part, it is worth noting that the only reason he had the money ready to loan in the first place was because John had given him warning that Hewitt's business was on the verge of going into bankruptcy, which enabled Bill to withdraw his $1000 interest in the firm before it went under. Furthermore, Bill told John that he "had always intended to give each of his children $1000 at age twenty-one"; yet the fact that John was a year short of that age apparently prompted his father to convert the promised gift into a loan. Throughout John's early adulthood, Bill Rockefeller often played games of this nature with his son, lending him money, demanding it back at short notice, then offering to loan it again. As an elderly man, Rockefeller credited his father with teaching him hard but necessary lessons about finance, but he would have been more than human if he had not felt some anger and disappointment over the fact that Bill treated him as little more than another reliable investment.

The firm of Clark and Rockefeller traded in "grain, fish, water, lime, plaster, coarse fine solar and dairy salt," according to the advertisements that went out after they opened their doors. By the end of their first year, the firm had earned a net profit of four thousand dollars. In 1859, the firm expanded. Rockefeller's name was dropped from the sign when he and Clark joined with another partner, George Gardner, who had once served as the mayor of Cleveland and had a substantial amount of capital to offer them. Rockefeller felt some injured pride over the loss of his status as equal partner in the firm, but his real outrage was reserved for the fact that Gardener and Clark both rejected Rockefeller's stern austerity. Rockefeller never made extravagant purchases even though he was making more money now, and he didn't think it appropriate when Gardener and Clark did either. When the two men bought a yacht, it annoyed Rockefeller so much that he refused their invitations to come and see it. "George Gardener," Rockefeller declared, "you're the most extravagant young man I ever knew! The idea of a young man like you, just getting a start in life, owning an interest in a yacht! You're injuring your credit at the banks—your credit and mine... No, I won't go on your yacht. I don't even want to see it." Gardener replied calmly, and his words give us some idea of how Rockefeller's contemporaries saw him back then: "John, I see that there are certain things on which you and I probably will never agree. I think you like money better than anything else in the whole world, and I do not. I like to have a little fun along with business as I go through life."

John was not entirely wrong, however, at least when it came to the banks and the firm's credit. It was John who was the successful borrower of the firm, not Clark or Gardener. Older men in the financial community approved of Rockefeller's regular habits and lack of vices; they had more confidence in him than they did in other men his age because of his standing in his church. Rockefeller's success as a borrower was key to his rapid success, because he was in constant need of large loans—not because his business wasn't making money, but because he had a hard time "obtain[ing] enough capital to do all the business I wanted to do and could do, given the necessary amount of money." The first large loan he was ever granted, for the sum of two thousand dollars, was given to him chiefly because the bank president was himself a staunch churchgoing man and had heard that John Rockefeller was a pillar of the Erie Street Mission church.

Civil War

In 1860, when John Rockefeller was 21 years old, Confederate soldiers in South Carolina fired on Union forces at Fort Sumter, and President Abraham Lincoln asked for 75,000 volunteers to enlist in the Union army to put the southern rebellion down. As a staunch lifelong abolitionist, and a resident of a city which helped smuggle many escaped slaves along the Underground Railroad to freedom in Canada, Rockefeller's sympathies were entirely with the

Union cause. But like many young men in the north who were wealthy, or at least had money to spare, John did not enlist in the army. "I wanted to go in the army and do my part," he said later, "But it was simply out of the question. We were in a new business, and if I had not stayed it must have stopped—and with so many dependent on it." Men of fighting age were excused from service if they were the sole source of support for their families. When John was eighteen, Bill Rockefeller had given him a sum of money and instructed him to build a house for his mother and four siblings. This was Bill's way of making a final, permanent provision for Eliza Davison and her children; from that point forward, he effectively washed his hands of any responsibility for them. In fact, far from providing for his family, he actually charged John rent for living in the house that John had built for him. It is therefore safe to say that John was the chief breadwinner in a family of six, and therefore could not possibly have gone to war. Three hundred dollars was the fee for hiring a substitute, and John paid his fee by outfitting a company of thirty men under the command of Captain Levi Scofield, a friend of Rockefeller's.

William Rockefeller also paid for a substitute, but their younger brother Frank was desperate to join the fighting, despite the fact that he had been turned away once because he was only fifteen years old. Frank begged John to give him the $75 he would need in order to be outfitted as a soldier, but John refused at first, telling him that he was a foolish boy and ought to be more concerned with getting his start in life than with indulging childish dreams of battlefield glory. Frank was determined to go to war, however. The next time he presented himself at the recruiting office, he wrote the number "18" on the soles of both his shoes, and when the recruiting officer asked his age, he boldly—and truthfully—declared that he was "*Over* 18, sir". In the end, John agreed to give him the money he needed, but the war would take a toll on

Frank Rockefeller that would last the rest of his life. His relationship with his brother John was destined to be troubled; he felt that he had "paid a severe price for heroism while John was rewarded for his self-aggrandizement. Ineffectual and full of self-pity, feeling cursed by bad luck, Frank envied his remarkable older brother, who seemed to succeed at every assignment and moved through his charmed business life with icily inexorable efficiency."

Despite the fact that the war drove a wedge between John and Frank Rockefeller, it proved a windfall for John's business. Commodities trading was at an all time high due to war time shortages. The Civil War bred a new appetite for wealth accumulation previously unknown in American society. Soldiers, mostly young men from small rural settlements who had never seen real cities before, traveled across the country by railroad where they were exposed to "luxury goods and urban sophistication" for the first time in their lives. Southerners, displaced by the devastation of the Union victory and more eager than ever to escape the oversight of federal government, migrated westward in large numbers, while northerners migrated south to take advantage of Reconstruction and the potential profits that lay in rebuilding a broken land. Businesses profited from war time government contracts. Rockefeller's firm quadrupled their profits during the war years due to inflation in commodities prices. This would provide John with the necessary capital to launch the next stage of his career, as he left behind trading in foodstuffs and began to venture into the industry that would make his legendary fortune: oil.

Chapter Three: Rockefeller & Andrews

"John D. Rockefeller saw a large and providential design in the discovery of Pennsylvania oil, stating that 'these vast stores of wealth were the gifts of the great Creator.' ...Rockefeller always viewed the industry through this rose-tinted spiritual lens, and it materially aided his success, for his conviction that God had given kerosene to suffering mankind gave him unswerving faith in the industry's future, enabling him to persist where less confident men stumbled and faltered."

> Ron Chernow, *Titan: The Life of John D. Rockefeller, Sr.*

Baffling as it will seem to those of us with a 21st century perspective, prior to 1850 or so, a farmer who found crude oil on his property tended to regard it as a nuisance rather than a goldmine.

Before crude oil was pumped out of the earth with derricks and sold for enormous sums to refineries, it was seen as a pollutant, an unpleasant scum that made well water and creeks undrinkable. Floating atop the surface of lakes and ponds with its greasy texture and iridescent hues, oil was useless to the average person. Certain Native American tribes had used it to make medicine, paint, and skin liniments, by floating blankets atop oil infested waters and wringing the oil-dense water out of the cloth again. Apart from this, a few peddling hucksters cut from the same cloth as Bill Rockefeller gathered up small quantities of "rock oil" and sold it as a medicine, claiming that it was cure for all sorts of ailments. But no one was interested in collecting crude oil in large quantities or trying to make anything useful out of it until the 1850's.

During the latter half of the 19th century, there was a burgeoning consumer need for illuminants—lighting, in other words. Poor women struggled to do needlework in the evenings, usually by the light of a single candle, which was placed in a saucer so that it could burn down into a puddle. So precious were candles that it was considered an important job perk for servants to be permitted to carry home the candle ends that their wealthy employers no longer had a use for. In poor homes, fireplaces usually provided the only illumination at home in the evenings, and since not every room had a fireplace, and not every family could afford to light multiple fires at a time, the entire family had to huddle in a single room. Reading was difficult, and any close work, like sewing, ruined a person's eyesight over time. Only the wealthy could afford to light their homes in the evenings on a nightly basis. The North American whaling industry provided sperm whale oil for lamps, which was said to give the cleanest, brightest light of any fuel available at the time, but after the Civil War, the demand for lighting outstripped what the whaling industry could supply. There were other lighting sources, including tallow, beeswax, even ordinary cooking fat, but the brightest lights were also the most likely to start dangerous fires, and the less dangerous lights provided poorer illumination.

It was for this reason—the overwhelming need for a cheap, safe, brightly burning source of light—that people began to investigate methods of pumping the crude oil out of Oil Creek in Pennsylvania, where the oil lay so heavy on the surface of the water that it was considered tainted. In the 1850s, the oil from Oil Creek was sent to a laboratory to be tested, in the hopes that it would prove a useful replacement for sperm oil and other illuminants. The chemist who performed the analysis discovered that once the oil had been refined, not only did it burn brightly, the byproducts created in the refining process were also commercially useful. The only problem was figuring out a means of gathering the crude oil on a large scale. Since the oil was clearly feeding into the lake from some fissure deep in the earth, it was determined that the oil might be extractable using a drilling process which was already being used to mine for salt. The Pennsylvania Rock-Oil company was accordingly formed to raise enough money to build the necessary equipment. Once the equipment was built, a complicated and time-consuming process in itself, "Colonel" Edwin Drake was hired by the Pennsylvania Rock-Oil Company to make use of it. He drilled for some time with no success, leading sniggering onlookers to refer to the lone oil derrick as "Drake's Folly". But in 1859, he at last succeeded in tapping a major vein of oil, sparking an oil rush in the rough backwoods country of western Pennsylvania. Prospectors scoured the countryside and bought up land wherever a potential source of oil lay, to the confusion of the property owners they were buying it from, who at first could not understand why anyone was willing to pay such large amounts of money for their land.

Oil would come to serve as the bedrock of John D. Rockefeller's fortune, but, ever the conservative, he was comparatively cautious about his investments while the industry was in its infancy. At first he traded oil only as another commodity, alongside the usual foodstuffs that Clark and Rockefeller specialized in. Then, an Englishman named Samuel Andrews, who worked in a lard-oil refinery in Cleveland, was given a barrel of crude oil to work with; eventually, he discovered the process of refining crude oil into kerosene, which was then a highly guarded secret. Andrews had essentially become one of the few owners of some of the most valuable intellectual property in America. The problem was figuring out how to use this knowledge to yield a commercial product—Samuels could not open a refinery without money, and he was neither a wealthy man nor a venture capitalist. As it happened, Andrews attended the same church as John Rockefeller, so the firm of Clark and Rockefeller was one of the first places where he made his pitch when he began searching for business partners. Andrews' initial interview was with Maurice Clark, who was less than enthusiastic; of the eight thousand dollars Andrews needed, Clark and Rockefeller could only give him $250. As soon as Andrews had finished talking to Clark, he barged into Rockefeller's office. John was much more interested in what Andrews had to say than his partner had been, and seemed favorably disposed towards making a large investment. Andrews returned to Clark's office, and when Clark heard that Rockefeller was enthusiastic, he decided to defer to his partner's judgment. In the end, Clark and Rockefeller invested four thousand dollars in Samuel Andrews' refinery, fully half the amount of money he needed. At the time, it seemed like a huge investment to Rockefeller, who did not yet foresee that oil would ever supersede food commodities as Clark and Rockefeller's main line of business.

Thanks to the investments of Rockefeller, Clark, and others, by the time the Civil War ended in 1864, the city of Cleveland was one of the chief centers of oil refinery in the country, alongside rural western Pennsylvania, Pittsburgh, and New York. Ida Tarbell's *History of Standard Oil Company*, an early masterpiece of investigative journalism published in serial form in *McClure's* magazine between 1902 and 1904, describes the transformation that the Oil Regions of Pennsylvania underwent after the process of refining crude oil into kerosene had been discovered:

"Twelve years before this strip of land had been but little better than a wilderness; its chief inhabitants the lumbermen, who every season cut great swaths of primeval pine and hemlock from its hills, and in the spring floated them down the Allegheny River to Pittsburgh. The great tides of Western emigration had shunned the spot for years as too rugged and unfriendly for settlement, and yet in twelve years this region avoided by men had been transformed into a bustling trade centre, where towns elbowed each other for place, into which three great trunk railroads had built branches, and every foot of whose soil was fought for by capitalists. It was the discovery and development of a new raw product, petroleum, which had made this change from wilderness to market-place. This product in twelve years had not only peopled a waste place of the earth, it had revolutionised the world's methods of illumination and added millions upon millions of dollars to the wealth of the United States."

In the 1860s, the first decade of the oil industry, the men who were pumping the oil from the earth were in a difficult position. The remote rural towns surrounding "Petrolia", as the Oil Regions were known, were scarcely commercial centers—most of them weren't reachable by railroad, and for the most part they didn't even have telegraph offices. The men who drilled the oil had to store it in leaky barrels and wait for representatives of the refineries to come to him before he could sell his product. These representatives went from oil well to oil well, on horseback where possible, though some areas were unreachable even by horse, due to the poor quality of the roads. The man with the oil had no choice but to sell it fairly cheaply, because the refinery representatives had to transport the oil themselves, so they could only buy and carry a little at a time, and the cost of their journey had to be deducted from the price of the product. The amount of oil available to the refineries at any given time was thus highly unstable, since they could only get their hands on as much oil as their representatives could convey to them, and this depended on the resourcefulness of the refinery agents, as well as weather and travel conditions. Investors in the oil business were thus speculators—any time they invested money, they were effectively making a bet as to how much oil would make its way back to the refineries in a given period. It was not until 1872, when new methods of extracting oil through pipelines were invented, that the process of conveying the oil from the wells to the refineries were regularized. A number of new railway stops were added to the oil regions, and as a result most of the buying and selling of oil took place on the trains themselves, as the oil men struggled to transport their barrels of crude oil to the railway stations to meet with the refinery representatives arriving by train.

At first, it was necessary to transport crude oil to refineries in far-away cities because it was virtually impossible to build refineries on the sites where the oil was being drilled. The infrastructure of a manufacturing city was needed to support the building of refineries, so cities like Pittsburgh, Philadelphia, and Baltimore handled the oil from Pennsylvania, while Cleveland refined most of the oil from

Kentucky. But there would be a significant financial advantage to refining the oil where it was being pumped, so attempts were made to bring the refining equipment to the Oil Regions by water. There were no wharfs or docks on the banks of the rivers leading to Pittsburgh, however, so getting the refinery equipment ashore often resulted in damage to the equipment. The process of transporting the equipment needed for a single refinery took weeks or months at a time. In addition to this, the chemicals used in the refinement process, along with the barrels to store all of these different liquids, had to be transported to the region as well. Again, the building of railroads in the area made this process far more efficient. Infrastructure was created so that the refining chemicals could be created on location, eliminating the need to transport them from the cities. By the early 1870s, the Pennsylvania oil country was producing about ten thousand barrels of oil a day, and the most profitable plants were the ones closest to the wells—only in

Cleveland and New York were the refineries larger and more productive. As the industry grew, more infrastructure grew up around it; transportation specialists set up business in the area, and the refineries began to produce more diverse products from the oil.

Rockefeller's refinery

"The chief refining competitor of Oil Creek in 1872 was Cleveland, Ohio. Since 1869 that city had done annually more refining than any other place in the country. Strung along the banks of Walworth and Kingsbury Runs, the creeks to which the city frequently banishes her heavy and evil-smelling burdens, there had been since the early sixties from twenty to thirty oil refineries. Why they were there, more than 200 miles from the spot where the oil was taken from the earth, a glance at a map of the railroads of the time will show: By rail and water Cleveland commanded the entire Western market. It had two trunk lines running to New York, both eager for oil traffic, and by Lake Erie and the canal it had for a large part of the year a splendid cheap waterway. Thus, at the opening of the oil business, Cleveland was destined by geographical position to be a refining center."

The above passage from Ida Tarbell's book describes John Rockefeller's first efforts at establishing dominion over the Cleveland refineries. Another biographer describes Kingsbury Run as "a three-acre parcel on the sloping, red-clay banks of a narrow waterway...which flowed into the Cuyahoga River and thus provided passage to Lake Erie, thus making it convenient to the new railroads. When John Rockefeller and Maurice Clark first went into business together, they had received a late shipment of beans which had partially spoiled during transport. John had picked through the entire shipment, bean by bean, separating the good from the bad. He brought the same painstaking energy to his Kingsbury Run refinery. He would often arrive at six in the morning to do chores for the cooper who made the barrels, nor did he shy from helping out with any other menial labor that needed doing. This hands-on approach to the business inspired him in lucrative ways. Because John understood every aspect of his business, his company began diversifying in order to streamline the refining process. Soon, Clark and Rockefeller was not only refining oil—they were also producing their own barrels and transporting their own equipment. By the end of their first year operating the refinery, oil had overtaken food commodities as Clark and Rockefeller's chief line of business.

Maurice Clark, John Rockefeller's business partner, remarked that John attended his refinery with a sort of loving attention to detail that he bestowed nowhere else in his life, save on

Erie Street Mission Baptist Church. Clark remarked, "John had abiding faith in two things—the Baptist creed and oil." One biographer describes Rockefeller during this period as a "very old, very young man" who "found boyish pleasure in doing business." Practically the only emotional outbursts anyone ever witnessed in him were the whoops of enthusiasm that could be heard from Rockefeller's office when he met with unexpected success in some matter of business. "The only time I ever saw John Rockefeller enthusiastic," remarked one business associate, "was when a report came in from the creek that his buyer had secured a cargo of oil at a figure much below the market price. He bounded from his chair with a shout of joy, danced up and down, hugged me, threw up his hat, acted so like a madman that I have never forgotten it." To call this a departure from Rockefeller's usual stoic, composed manner would be understating matters greatly.

Rockefeller first visited the Oil Regions of Pennsylvania personally in 1861. The infrastructure springing up around the wells had given rise to "a sort of gold-field rush", as Rockefeller himself described it. "Great fortunes were made by some of the first adventurers, and everything was carried on in a sort of helter-skelter way." The boomtowns that had risen up around the oil wells were violent, chaotic settlements where hardworking men manned the oil derricks all day, only to lose their money gambling and get into fights over women at night. One of these settlements was actually nicknamed "Sodden Gomorrah", due to the muddy roads and the prevalence of prostitution, hard drinking, and gambling found there. This was bound to horrify a staunch Baptist like John Rockefeller, who eschewed all such fleshly vices; such working conditions cried out to be brought under the heel of disciplined commerce. It would not be precisely accurate to say that Rockefeller set about rationalizing, streamlining, and ordering the oil industry in order to save men from the snares of sin, but there was certainly something messianic about his attitude. He wanted to save the oil industry from itself, for the good of everyone, producers, refiners, and customers alike. But when he turned a deaf ear to every protest from the Oil Region itself, which did not want to be "saved" by a man like Rockefeller, it was in part because he thought that men of such dissolute character and habits were not capable of judging what was best for them.

End of a partnership

By 1865, John Rockefeller's relationship with Maurice Clark, and his brothers, who were also partners in the firm, was souring. He felt that they looked down on him as a mere bookkeeper because he devoted so much time to the company ledgers. They considered Rockefeller prudish, a "Sunday-school superintendent" whose severe morality annoyed them nearly as much as his audacious borrowing. Rockefeller was intent on expanding the business by leaps and bounds, and for that he needed capital. The Clarks did not share this vision, and felt he was taking unjustifiable business risks. But Rockefeller had little respect for their judgment. He considered their habits dissolute and grandiose, and he was on the lookout for an opportunity to break away from them. Ron Chernow writes that Rockefeller "wanted to be surrounded by trustworthy people who could inspire confidence in customers and bankers alike. He drew a characteristic conclusion: The weak, immoral man was also destined to be a poor businessman. Rockefeller himself, speaking to a journalist about his early partnership with the Clark brothers, explained that by 1865, "we were beginning to prosper and I felt very uneasy at my name being linked up with these speculators."

Those who saw him as little more than a mild-mannered bookkeeper were often surprised to discover that John Rockefeller was capable of great boldness. His decisions struck onlookers as all the more audacious because he kept his own counsel, mulling over his options in the privacy of his own head for weeks or months at a time before making a move. All the same, when Rockefeller dissolved his partnership with the Clark brothers, the last people it ought to have surprised were the Clarks themselves, because every time they disagreed with Rockefeller over some aspect of the business, they threatened to cut ties with him and go their own way. To the Clarks, these were only idle threats, meant to bring Rockefeller in line, but to Rockefeller, they represented an opportunity. He wanted to be rid of them, but he couldn't simply pack up his bags and leave. Only if the firm dissolved and went up for auction could Rockefeller buy his partners out and steer the firm in the direction it needed go. A unanimous vote of all five partners—the three Clarks, Rockefeller, and Samuel Andrews—

was needed to formally dissolve the firm. One night, Rockefeller invited the Clark brothers to his house for dinner and announced that he wanted to take out a huge new bank loan. On cue, each of the Clarks declared that if Rockefeller was going to keep on this way, it would be better if the firm were to break up. What they did not realize was that Rockefeller had made the announcement on purpose in order to goad them into saying as much. He had already gone to Andrews in secret, explaining that he wanted the two of them to shake the Clarks off and go into business together; all he needed in order to accomplish this was for the Clarks to reaffirm their desire to dissolve the firm and for Andrews to make the vote unanimous. Andrews agreed to support him, so the morning after the dinner, Rockefeller went directly to the newspapers and placed an announcement that the firm was dissolving and going up for auction. The Clark brothers were astonished—for all their threats, Rockefeller had never given them any indication that he wanted to break the firm up. But Rockefeller assured them he was serious, so Maurice Clark agreed to the auction.

On the day of the auction, Maurice Clark showed up with a lawyer, while Rockefeller came alone. The bids escalated five hundred dollars at a time, until at last Clark capitulated. Rockefeller himself described the auction's conclusion:

"Finally it advanced to $60,000, and by slow stages to $70,000, and I almost feared for my ability to buy the business and have the money to pay for it. At last the other side bid $72,000. Without hesitation I said $72,500. Mr. Clark then said: 'I'll go no higher, John; the business is yours.' 'Shall I give you a check for it now?' I suggested. 'No,' Mr. Clark said, 'I'm glad to trust you for it; settle at your convenience.'"

Rockefeller later declared to a journalist that "It was the day that determined my career. I felt the bigness of it, but I was as calm as I am talking to you now." He paid a steep financial price to be the head of his own company, but his victory at the auction meant that, at the age of twenty-five, he was in sole charge of one of the largest oil refineries in the entire world. The firm was rechristened Rockefeller & Andrews.

Ida Tarbell describes the effect which Rockefeller had on the industry once he had a firm of his own to helm:

"In the new firm Andrews attended to the manufacturing. The pushing of the business, the buying and the selling, fell to Rockefeller. From the start his effect was tremendous. He had the frugal man's hatred of waste and disorder, of middlemen and unnecessary manipulation, and he began a vigorous elimination of these from his business. The residuum that other refineries let run into the ground, he sold. Old iron found its way to the junk shop. He bought his oil directly from the wells. He made his own barrels. He watched and saved and contrived. The ability with which he made the smallest bargain furnishes topics to Cleveland story-tellers to-day. Low-voiced, soft-footed, humble, knowing every point in every man's business, he never tired until he got his wares at the lowest possible figure. "John always got the best of the bargain," old men tell you in Cleveland to-day, and they wince though they laugh in telling it. 'Smooth, and a savvy fellow,' is their description of him. To drive a good bargain was the

joy of his life."

Marriage

John D. Rockefeller first made the acquaintance of the woman he was to marry while they were both students at Central High School in Cleveland. Laura Celestia Spelman, called Cettie by her friends and family, was, like most students at the school, a member of a prosperous, respectable, well-heeled family, several rungs higher on the social ladder than the Rockefeller family, which, though helmed by the rigidly respectable Eliza Davison Rockefeller, felt the shadow of Bill's bigamy and fraud hovering over them like a moral and social contagion.

Though it was something of a tradition for Rockefeller men to marry women who were considered to be above them, in that they were better educated and from more respectable families, John was acutely aware that his father and grandfather had done so to their wives' suffering and unhappiness. Like Godfrey and Bill Rockefeller, John had his sights set on a woman whose family was wealthier and had better standing in the community than his, but *he* would not offer himself to Cettie until he had made something of himself. Only when he was position to offer his wife a considerable degree of security would he marry. It might be said that John was determined to make himself into a good investment, one that Cettie would have no cause to regret.

On John's side, there was no doubt whatsoever that Cettie was the one woman in the world best able to make him happy and support him in his life's work. Cettie was intelligent, steady, good-humored—she was even a student of business in her own right. From the time they were teenagers, she knew about John's business ambitions, and she encouraged him to do all that was necessary to make a success of himself. She was the perfect match for him, and he was determined to make himself the perfect match for her. For this reason, even though his heart had been fixed on Cettie since they were sixteen, he waited nine years before he proposed to her— the same nine-year period which spanned from his first job search at sixteen to the day he became the head of Rockefeller & Andrews at 25. Throughout this period, John and Cettie remained friends, and all the while she kept a weather eye on his progress. Cettie's family had been wealthy once, but had lost most of their money, through no fault of their own, in a bank collapse. The Spelman family fortunes had recovered somewhat, but they were no longer as rich as they had been before. Cettie thus regarded it as her duty to marry a man who could offer security not only to her but to her whole family, just in case fortune should turn against them again. Far from considering Cettie grasping or a gold-digger, John considered this nothing less than plain common sense on her part.

Ron Chernow, drawing from the reminiscences of Cettie's sister Lucy (called "Lute"), describes the qualities that made Cettie Spelman the ideal match for John:

"It is hard to picture a young woman more perfectly suited to John D. Rockefeller's values than the sensible, cheerful Laura Celestia Spelman, who share his devotion to duty and thrift. They ratified each other's views about the fundamentals of life... Her mild surface belied an adamantine determination. She was 'gentle and lovely, but resolute with indomitable will'," noted her sister Lucy... 'There was a persuasion in her touch as she laid her fingers ever so gently on your arm... She was full of mirth and cheer, yet...rather inclined to be grave and reserved."

In addition to all this, John and Cettie had in common an unswerving Christian faith. Like John, Cettie's social life centered entirely around the church. Cettie was descended from the Puritans of Plymouth Bay, and ascetic Christianity was in her blood, as it was in John's, via his mother and grandmother. John and Cettie shared passionate beliefs in temperance and abolitionism. The Spelman household served as a stop on the Underground Railroad, ferrying escaped slaves to freedom further north. The famous preacher, abolitionist, and suffragist Sojourner Truth was one of the former slaves they harbored. Cettie once remarked that the only time she had ever seen her mother cooking dinner on a Sunday—a day on which the family normally ate cold leftovers, since all forms of work were prohibited on the Sabbath—was to make hot meals for the refugee slaves who were preparing to embark on the long journey to Canada. Cettie's interests were not restricted to religion only, however; she had a variety of cultured interests, including art, music, and literature. John also enjoyed music and had even entertained the possibility of becoming a pianist for a brief time in his boyhood. He and Cettie often played duets together.

In her youth, Cettie was a proud first-wave feminist, just coming into maturity after

Elizabeth Cady Stanton and Lucretia Mott organized the Seneca Falls Convention, advocating for women's suffrage. As the valedictorian of her graduating high school class, she delivered a speech entitled "I Can Paddle My Own Canoe". Her speech "chided men for depriving women of culture then hypocritically blaming them for their dependency." She wrote, "But give woman culture—let her thread the many paths of science—allow mathematics and exact thought on all subjects to exert their influence on her mind and conventions need not trouble her about her 'proper sphere'." Cettie's belief in women's ability to make their own way in the world was more than just adolescent grandstanding; when her family moved to Iowa, she and her sister Lute remained in Cleveland, and studied at Oread Collegiate Institute, one of the first institutions of higher learning in the United States to admit women. At Oread, Cettie ran the campus literary magazine and published articles about "the three aristocracies then ruling America—an aristocracy of intellect in New

England, wealth in the Atlantic states, and blood in the South." Later Cettie and Lute studied music at the Cleveland Institute and afterwards took jobs as school teachers. Her family's financial situation at the time made it necessary that she work to support herself, but it was a necessity she did not resent. In fact, she was so pleased with her career that it began to seem unimportant to her whether she ever married at all. But she was corresponding occasionally with Rockefeller during this period, and she was aware that his intentions towards her were of a serious matrimonial bent. "I seem to have no anxiety about a life of single-blessedness," she told her former music teacher, but "a gentleman told me not long ago, that he was in no particular rush to have me get married, but he hoped that in the multitude of my thoughts I would not forget the subject." Since female teachers were only allowed to work for as long as they remained single, marriage to Rockefeller would mean an end to her career.

After Rockefeller established his Cleveland oil refinery, he began taking Cettie on drives along the water, pointing out the details of the operation. Her remarks on the subject never failed to interest him. "Her judgment was always better than mine," he once claimed. "She was a woman of great sagacity. Without her keen advice, I would be a poor man." John was a patient man in love just as he was in business, but in early 1864 another suitor for Cettie's hand appeared on the scene, and John began to grow nervous. Finally, in March of that year, he went to Cettie and proposed, in a manner suited to both their personalities: "John D. wanted to marry her, so he went to her one day and proposed in a business-like way, just like he would make a business proposition. She accepted him in the same business-like way." To seal the deal, Rockefeller made the most extravagant purchase of his life up to that point, in the form of a diamond engagement ring which cost over a hundred dollars. The purpose of this extravagance was to demonstrate to Cettie and her family that he was now in a position to provide amply for a wife and family. It must have impressed the senior Spelmans, because Cettie and John were married six months later, in the fall of 1864, in a small ceremony in the Spelman home. Having proved his point with the engagement ring, he spent a mere fifteen dollars on the wedding ring. The newlyweds took a month for their honeymoon, and afterwards moved in with John's mother for six months, until they located an appropriate house in their price range. John was doing well enough by this point to live in a fairly grand style, but it suited the personalities of both bride and groom to live modestly, so they took no servants.

John D. Rockefeller's marriage, together with the formation of the Rockefeller & Andrews company, marked the end of his youthful struggle to establish himself in the world. From

1865 forward, his life would run on rails, with no uncertainty and no setbacks on the path towards fantastic wealth and domination in the oil industry. He was one of the most peculiarly single-minded men imaginable, and now there were no more distractions in his way. In shaking off his association with the Clark brothers he had freed himself of encumbrances in his business life, and in marrying Laura Spelman he had acquired the support he needed in his domestic life. Nothing stood in his path now; for the next twenty-five years, he would devote all his energy to the cause of organizing the oil industry and becoming the richest man in history in the process.

Chapter Four: Rockefeller, Andrews, and Flagler

Transportation

Prior to the Civil War, most people lit their homes with lamps that ran on an illuminant oil called camphene, derived from turpentine. But the major suppliers of turpentine were located in the American south, which lay in shambles after its defeat by the Union. The war had similarly disrupted the whaling industry, and as a result, the need for kerosene was now greater than it had ever been. Before the war, it was said that cotton was king in American commerce. After the war, kerosene took its place. Byproducts created during the process of refining crude oil into kerosene included benzene, paraffin, and petroleum jelly, all of them commercially valuable, and Rockefeller's Standard Works—the name given to Rockefeller & Andrews after it acquired a second refinery—dealt in all of them.

Curiously, the only by-product they had no use for was gasoline; prior to the invention of automobiles it was considered useless. Gasoline was usually discarded by being poured onto the ground, where it seeped into the ground and polluted the water. Long before the damaging effects of such pollutants on the environment were understood, people learned to fear the threat of gasoline-soaked mud and water. Steamboat captains dared not shovel their coal overboard, as had previously been their habit, for fear of setting the water itself ablaze with the hot cinders. By 1869 the supply of kerosene was so plentiful that it outstripped demand, but a single well or refinery could be wiped out in an instant by fire. So many people lost their investments— and occasionally, their lives—in oil fires that in Oil Creek signs were posted announcing that "Smokers Will Be Shot". Rockefeller himself was in a permanently anxious state lest fire break out in his own refineries.

In the first decades after oil was discovered in Pennsylvania, another fear beset the industry: what if the supply of oil was limited? What if all the wells suddenly dried up? As far as anyone knew, the American Midwest and mid-Atlantic was the only source of oil in the world, and no one could guess how much of it lay beneath the earth. Rockefeller was not immune to anxiety on this score—he often lay awake at night, wondering what would happen if the oil fields gave out. But whenever he considered pulling out of the business, he was comforted by his genuine conviction that oil had been given as a gift by God to men, and as such, it would prove a stable source of light for the world and revenue for his business for many years to come. Wall Street bankers, on the other hand, did not share his conviction. Rockefeller again faced the perennial difficulty of gaining as much capital as he needed to do all the business he was capable of doing, and his needs were larger than the

Cleveland banks could supply. Wall Street had the money he needed, but the specters of fire and dry wells made them regard the oil business as nothing short of speculation—dependable investments like railroads and government contracts were their bread and butter. By this point, John had formed a partnership with his young brother William, and it was William he sent to New York to wheedle capital out of the tightfisted New York financiers. William was better suited to this task than John—he had their father's congenial manners and easy way with people, and he had an easier time talking people into giving him what he wanted than the sober, straight-laced John. And yet John's reputation for meticulous honesty helped him on Wall Street just as it had helped him as a younger man getting his start in Cleveland.

One biographer writes of this period that "It is impossible to comprehend Rockefeller's breathtaking ascent without realizing that he always moved into battle backed by abundant cash. Whether riding out downturns or coasting on booms, he kept plentiful reserves and won many bidding contests simply because his war chest was deeper." He also had a knack for winning the trust of bankers by never appearing too eager to get his hands on their money. If he needed $5000, he circulated the rumor that he was in need of $10,000. On one occasion, when he was sorely in need of $15,000, a banker spontaneously offered him $50,000. This was a windfall unimagined in his wildest dreams, but Rockefeller nonetheless asked the banker if he might have 24 hours to think it over first. Even bankers who were skeptical about oil were not skeptical about Rockefeller himself.

Ida Tarbell's history of Standard Oil summarizes the personalities involved in the company in its earliest days. Compared to Rockefeller's later accounts, she assigns a more significant role to Samuel Andrews than Rockefeller gives him credit for, but her assessment of William Rockefeller tallies with every known account of him:

"Not only did Mr. Rockefeller control the largest firm in this most prosperous centre of a prosperous business, he controlled one of amazing efficiency. The combination, in 1870, of the various companies with which he was connected had brought together a group of remarkable men. Samuel Andrews, by all accounts, was the ablest mechanical superintendent in Cleveland. William Rockefeller, the brother of John D. Rockefeller, was not only an energetic and intelligent business man, he was a man whom people liked. He was open-hearted, jolly, a good story-teller, a man who knew and liked a good horse not too pious, as some of John's business associates thought him, not a man to suspect or fear, as many a man did John. Old oil men will tell you on the creek to-day how much they liked him in the days when he used to come to Oil City buying oil for the Cleveland firm. The personal quality of William Rockefeller was, and always has been, a strong asset of the Standard Oil Company.

"Probably the strongest man in the firm after John D. Rockefeller was Henry M. Flagler. He was, like the others, a young man, and one who, like the head of the firm, had the passion for money, and in a hard self-supporting experience, begun when but a boy, had learned, as well as his chief, some of the principles of making it. He was untiring in his efforts to increase the business, quick to see an advantage, as quick to take it. He had no scruples to make him hesitate over the ethical quality of a contract which was advantageous. Success, that is, making money, was its own justification. He was not a secretive man, like John D. Rockefeller, not a dreamer, but he could keep his mouth shut when necessary and he knew the worth of a financial dream when it was laid before him. It must have been evident to every business man who came in contact with the young Standard Oil Company that it would go far. The firm itself must have known it would go far. Indeed nothing could have stopped the Standard Oil Company in 1870 the oil business being what it was but an entire change in the nature of the members of the firm, and they were not the kind of material which changes."

Ida Tarbell, who pioneered investigative journalism, was the first person to look into Rockefeller's personal history, and the first to seriously research the origins of the Standard Oil company. There were many unauthorized biographies written about Rockefeller during his lifetime, virtually all of them uncritical and adulatory, more focused on the quintessentially American myth of Rockefeller as the self-made millionaire than on any serious evaluation of his business practices. Such books therefore made no mention of Bill Rockefeller's frauds and schemes, or his bigamous marriage, nor did they investigate the practices that led to Standard Oil crushing all competition to become the "mother of monopoly" in the United States. Rockefeller prided himself on never holding grudges, but the mere mention of Ida Tarbell's name could bring an angry gleam to his eye, even when he was a very old man. He dismissed her writing as slanderous, idle words from a "poison tongue". But while he quibbled over her portrayal of his family history, and vehemently contradicted the aspersions she cast on his motivations, he could not dispute certain basic facts.

For instance: when the oil industry was divided into competing camps, with the Oil Regions of Pennsylvania pitted against the big refineries in Cleveland and New York, Rockefeller clung to his refineries on Kingsbury Run for one important reason. Transporting the oil from the wells to the refineries was the most expensive and uncertain aspect of the industry. The owner of a well had to undertake transportation costs for his product on his own. Since he rarely had the horses and wagons needed to carry all that his well had produced, he more often relied on roving teams of wagon drivers, called teamsters, to get his oil barrels to the railroads and the refineries. Because the teamsters charged high prices for their services, the owners of the wells looked for other means to transport the oil, leading to the invention of the first oil pipelines. But the teamsters destroyed as many of the early pipelines as they could in order to keep the well owners dependent on them. Eventually, everyone would use pipelines, but until then, the refineries that could wrangle the cheapest rates from the railroads made the most money.

This was what made Kingsbury Run so essential to Rockefeller's early success. There were three major railroads positioned near Kingsbury Run: the New York Central, the Erie Railroad, and the Pennsylvania Railroad. Each of these three railroads were eager for Rockefeller's business, as Rockefeller's refinery was producing over twice as many barrels as any other refinery in the world at the time. Moreover, during the spring and summer thaws, Rockefeller could bypass the railroads altogether and transport by water along the Erie Canal. This put him in a good position to negotiation cheap rates from the railroads, rates that no other refinery owner was able to get, as Ida Tarbell discovered some forty years later when she began interviewing Rockefeller's former competitors. Other oil men would confront the railroads, demanding to know why Rockefeller's oil was traveling at one rate and theirs at another; the railroad would inform them that they were also eligible for the same rebates Rockefeller was getting, but when the rebates were applied for, the money mysteriously failed to appear.

The Lake Shore Deal

In the 1870s, there was a great deal of competitive resentment from the Oil Regions of Pennsylvania towards the Cleveland refineries. It seemed to the well owners and refineries of Petrolia that western Pennsylvania had a natural right to "refine for the whole world". After all, that was where the oil was being drilled, and that was where the owners of the wells lived. The distance between the wells and the east coast refineries was much shorter; it seemed to them that the Cleveland refineries had only achieved greater production levels by some sort of dirty trick. Given time, the creek refineries felt that they would, in Tarbell's words, reign over "an oil kingdom which eventually should handle the entire business and compel Cleveland and Pittsburgh either to abandon their works or bring them to the oil country." They were encouraged in this ambition by the Pennsylvania Railroad company, the railroad best positioned to do business with the Oil Creek refineries.

The Pennsylvania Railroad, eager to wipe out its competitors, began charging extortionate rates to carry oil to refineries in Pittsburgh. This was merely a first step; the railroad's ultimate goal was that Cleveland should be "wiped out as a refining center as with a sponge". In a panic, the Cleveland refineries began making plans to transfer their centers of operation to the Oil Regions of Pennsylvania, leaving the Erie and New York Central Railroads flailing to make up the lost business. Rockefeller, who took the threats made by the Pennsylvania Railroad as a spur to action, rather than as a sign that it was time to abandon ship, promptly made a secret deal with railroad magnate Jay Gould to form the Alleghany Transportation Company, described as "the first major pipeline network serving Oil Creek". Rockefeller, and his partner Flagler, also worked out a deal with the New York Central railroad, in which Rockefeller and his partners agreed to assume liability for fire or accidents occurring during transport, agreed to stop transporting their refined oil by water during the summers, and most importantly, agreed to transport sixty carloads of refined oil by rail every day. (Sixty carloads a day was a great deal more than Rockefeller's refineries were producing at the time, but Rockefeller was planning to coordinate with the other Cleveland refineries to make up the difference.) In return for all these incentives, the railroad agreed to transport crude oil from Pennsylvania to Kingsbury Run, and then transport the refined oil from Cleveland to New York, for a mere $1.65 per barrel. The going rate was then $2.40 per barrel.

This arrangement, afterwards called the Lake Shore Deal, marked a turning point not only in Rockefeller's personal fortunes, but in the way that business was done in America. The railroad companies would come to see that economies of scale worked greatly to their advantage, and for this reason, it was in their interest to promote monopolies of every commodity being sold in the

United States. Later historians of business, beginning with Ida Tarbell, would see this point as the moment at which Rockefeller ceased to be a clever and enterprising young businessman and became a cheating, free-dealing crook that made life impossible for small businesses to thrive in America. Rockefeller never saw himself in this light, of course. When he was in his nineties, Rockefeller was informed by a journalist named William O. Inglis that Tarbell had accused him of "threatening to crush rivals who refused to join his cartel" in 1872. Hearing this accusation prompted a rare display of fury from Rockefeller. Inglis describes the scene:

"'That is absolutely false!' exclaimed Mr. Rockefeller so loudly that I looked up from the notes. As he spoke he jumped up from the big chair in which he was reclining and walked over to my table. His face was flushed and his eyes were burning. It was the first time I had ever seen him show any but pleasant feeling, and there could be no doubt that he was aflame with anger and resentment. His voice rang out loud and clear. He did not beat the desk with his fist, but stood there with his hands clenched, controlling himself with evident effort. 'That is absolutely false!' he cried, 'and no man was told that by me or by any of our representatives. You may put that down once and for all. That statement is an absolute lie.'"

Later in the course of Inglis's interview, Rockefeller returned to this theme. "How ridiculous all that talk is! It's twaddle, poisonous twaddle, put out for a purpose. As a matter of fact, we were all in a sinking ship, if existing cut-throat competition continued, and we were trying to build a lifeboat to carry us all to the shore. You don't have to threaten men to get them to leave a sinking ship in a lifeboat."

Yet even if Rockefeller did not suffer any pangs of conscience, either in 1872 or later, the secrecy surrounding his actions reveal some degree of awareness that others might take a dimmer view of his machinations. The rebate arrangement he made with the railroad, for instance, was a handshake deal, the details never committed to paper. Furthermore, Rockefeller was always careful to point out that the transportation deal had chiefly been the work of his partner Flagler—he was both giving credit where credit was due and distancing himself from the one area of business where he was liable to attract the most criticism, the railroad rebates.

Largely forgotten today, now that railroads have long ceased to be the primary means of transporting goods across the United States, railroad rebates were granted freely to large businesses in the years after the Civil War in an effort to recoup the war time losses the railroads had suffered. These rebates came to be regarded as immoral, a shady trick, towards the latter end of the 19th century, but they were a common method of doing business in 1872. Not until the Interstate Commerce Act of 1887 did railroad rebates become technically illegal, and not until 1903 did they cease entirely. The grounds for their illegalization rested in the fact that the railroads had been given the right of eminent domain in order to expand across the country—that is, a railroad could force a private landowner to sell their property so that railroad tracks could be built across it. Technically, such rights are only granted to companies that somehow serve the common good; the 21st century equivalent would be a highway, open to the use of anyone owning or riding in a motor vehicle. Ida Tarbell was among the first to point out that it can only be unethical for a large business which has been given special rights by the government so that it can serve the common good to make secret deals with other large businesses for their own profit. But it is also worth remembering that in 1872, this was uncharted territory, both in business and law. The illegalization of monopolies, along with most of our ethical expectations for big businesses, arose from the battles that were fought during this period of American history.

Millionaire's Row

If not yet a millionaire himself, Rockefeller's fortunes were now such that he could afford a home on Euclid Avenue in Cleveland, touted as the most beautiful street in the world, and home to many families that were very wealthy indeed. The Rockefellers' new home was not especially grand in comparison to those of their neighbors, but this had less to do with what they could afford to spend and more to do with the fact that Rockefeller liked fixer-uppers—he wanted big rooms with high ceilings, and plenty of yard space where he could landscape his own garden and build stables and coach houses, but luxuries were anathema to him. His favorite and most expensive hobby was racing horses, and it was said that the stables he built for Midnight, Flash, Jesse, Baron, and Trifle to live in was even grander than the house he had built for himself.

Rockefeller's domestic life with Cettie was boringly, happily conventional in every respect—in no way was John Rockefeller more unlike his father Bill than when it came to his relationship with his family. Rockefeller came home at the end of the day to spend the evenings with his wife, and later their children; when they felt like socializing, they attended performances at the Philharmonic or hosted dinners for their small circle of friends, who were largely church acquaintances. This was partly due to their own retiring natures, and partly due to their strict temperance views—a serious temperance man in those days would not so much as dine in a restaurant that served alcohol, any more than he would partake of it himself. Since these views were scarcely shared by society as a whole, there were only so many places the Rockefellers could safely go without being affronted by the sight of a beer bottle.

Anyone studying Rockefeller's youth, particularly his first decade in business, could be forgiven for assuming that he was a workaholic by nature, but this was not the case. After he had moved to Euclid Avenue, he began spending less and less time at the firm, installing a telegraph line that connected his house to his offices so he could stay at home and still be reached in case anything urgently needed his attention. Rockefeller claimed that this was the secret to his enormous productivity: by resting and pacing himself, he kept his energies up, his mind clear, and preserved his health. It is hard to argue with this prescription, considering that he lived well into his nineties.

The Rockefeller's eldest child, Bessie, was born in 1866, when they were still living at the house on Cheshire Street. They were to have four more children, all born in the Euclid Avenue house. Their second daughter, Alice, was born in 1869, but she died when she was only two years old. The other three, Alta, Edith, and John Jr., were all born between 1871 and 1874. Remarkably, Cettie Rockefeller was attended at the birth of all of her children by Dr. Myra Herrick, the first female doctor in Cleveland. Herrick would later operate a free medical clinic for poor women staffed by other female doctors, and the Rockefellers were among the clinic's chief financial supporters.

By all reports, Rockefeller was an excellent father. Again, it was as if the specter of Bill Rockefeller lay constantly before him, in all ways an example of how not to behave. Rockefeller spent as much time with his family as possible, and unlike most Victorian fathers, he did not shirk his share of childcare duties, even when the children were babies and at their most demanding. He was soft-spoken, playful, and performed tricks to keep the children amused. From their father, the Rockefeller children learned how to swim, row a boat, skate on frozen ponds, and ride horses and bicycles, the latter being a fairly new invention.

At the same time, the Rockefellers kept their children confined to the house in a way that struck some visitors as unnatural. The children didn't attend school, but were instead educated at home by governesses. They were allowed to have friends come to visit them at their house for a week or two at a time, but they were never allowed to leave home and return the visit. Rockefeller's son, John Jr., recalled that, "We had no childhood friends, and no school friends." It was undoubtedly the Rockefeller's religious beliefs that gave rise to their children's cloistered existence. Considering that Rockefeller had to investigate the site of a picnic ground for the presence of discarded beer bottles before he would accept an invitation to attend a barbecue, it is scarcely surprising that they kept their children, especially their daughters, as sheltered from "worldly" influences as they could possibly manage. Amongst evangelical Christians today, there are still many families who live a similarly cloistered lifestyle, homeschooling their children and restricting their social activities to church events. The Rockefellers were an early example of this trend.

Eager that their children should not grow up spoiled simply because their father was wealthy, the Rockefellers instilled the values of thrift and self-denial in them from an early age. When Rockefeller suggested buying the children a bicycle apiece, Cettie insisted that he buy only one, because then the children would have to learn how to share. Cettie once shocked one of her female acquaintances by declaring that a girl only really needed two dresses, a plain one for everyday wear and a smarter one for church. All of the children were dressed in hand-me-down clothing—even John Jr., who as a very young child wore only dresses, because his older siblings were all girls. Rockefeller wanted to encourage his children to develop keen financial instincts, so instead of giving them a set allowance, he paid set rates for specific household chores. Once, when one of his daughters was accompanying him on a train ride, he told a colleague, "This little girl is earning money already. You never could imagine how she does it. I have learned what my gas bills should average when the gas is managed with care, and I have told her that she can have for pin money all that she will save every month on this mount, so she goes around every night and keeps the gas turned down where it is not needed." In addition to all this, Rockefeller made certain that his children did not fully understand, until they were adults, precisely how wealthy their family was. It was his view that he had developed a talent for finance because he had learned how to be thrifty out of necessity when he was a boy. His own children were never permitted to do without things that they needed, but when it came to luxuries, he saw to it that they earned and budgeted for them.

As to Cettie Rockefeller, her marriage to John continued to be harmonious, utterly without quarrels or disagreements. But whereas John continued to mingle with the outside world, which inevitably broadened his perspectives, marriage changed Cettie from a nascent bluestocking who championed the enlarging social and professional sphere of women, into a kind but narrow woman whose intellectual interests ranged no further than what was necessary to mold her children into morally upright adults. She could easily have afforded an entire complement of household staff, but even when the hired two housemaids, she continued to do the bulk of the housework herself. After

Cettie's marriage, her sister Lute came to live with the family and help look after the children. Lute, by contrast to her sister, was widely read and not so rigid in her religious principles as Cettie and John, and it was she who exposed the children to a wider world of ideas, more complex than the threadbare maxims that formed the basis of their mother's teachings.

Chapter Five: Standard Oil

Cooperation vs Competition

By later 1869, the oil industry had hit a slump. There were more refineries by now than there was crude oil waiting to be refined into kerosene, and approximately 90% of all refineries were losing money on their operations. In this dire state of affairs, a man named John H. Alexander, who operated a rival refinery in Cleveland, offered to sell his business to Rockefeller at a tenth of its value. The slump had affected Rockefeller's operations as well, and for a time it seemed to him that all the success he had accrued over the last decade was likely to be lost. But he retained his abiding faith that oil was God's gift to mankind, and this saw him through the crisis. He was an optimist at heart, so while the oil industry appeared to be crashing around his ears, he looked for the opportunities in the midst of the chaos. As one biographer states: "He saw that his individual success as a refiner was now menaced by an industrywide failure and that it therefore demanded a systemic solution." So he began to take the industry in hand—with huge consequences for American business. Cooperation, not competition, was the key, to Rockefeller's way of thinking. Other people felt that his goal was to crush competitors, not cooperate with them.

The chief problem was the excess of refineries. According to prevailing economic theories of the day, the owners and operators of refineries should have been internally motivated to abandon their operations as the price of kerosene plummeted. Instead, infected by dreams of fantastic overnight wealth, they continued to drill, and continued to build refineries, despite the fact that they weren't making any money off them. There was, in short, more competition than the market could support, and every operation in the industry was being damaged as a result. The solution, as Rockefeller devised it, was "a giant cartel that would reduce overcapacity, stabilize prices, and rationalize the industry." Something similar had already been tried amongst the Oil Creek refineries themselves during the Civil War, which were now organized under the name of the Petroleum Producers' Association.

Rockefeller's strategy was to buy up as many of the small refineries as he possibly could so that production could be capped at levels the market could bear. But in order to do this, he would need vast amounts of capital, more than he had ever raised before. It was his business partner, Henry Flagler, who came up with the solution: the firm should incorporate and start selling shares to investors. Thus, Rockefellers, Andrew, and Flagler was dissolved and the Standard Oil Company of Ohio was formed, with John D. Rockefeller as its president. From the beginning, it was the largest joint-stock company in the world, with capital of more than a million dollars. Standard Oil, Rockefeller confidently predicted, would one day "refine all the oil and make all the barrels". Neither Rockefeller nor any of the other company officers drew a salary—the money they made depended, like the rest of their investors, on the success of their investments. But of course, Rockefeller owned the largest number of shares, and continued to buy as many as he could afford.

The Cleveland Massacre

"For his admirers, 1872 was the annus mirabilis of John D. Rockefeller's life, while for his critics it constituted the darkest chapter. The year revealed both his finest and most problematic qualities as a businessman: his visionary leadership, his courageous persistence, his capacity to think in strategic terms, but also his lust for domination, his messianic self-righteousness, and his contempt for those shortsighted mortals who made the mistake of standing in his way. What rivals saw as a naked power grab, Rockefeller regarded as a heroic act of salvation, nothing less than the rescue of the oil business."

Ron Chernow

In 1871, Rockefeller purchased Bostwick and Tilford, one of New York's chief firms dealing in refined oil. The purchase was made secretly, a private arrangement between Rockefeller and Jabez Bostwick, who shared Rockefeller's strict Baptist principles. Rockefeller liked to operate in secret, and he saw nothing shady or unethical about doing so. His critics would disagree, particularly after January 1, 1872. Standard Oil greeted the New Year with several new investors onboard, tripling the company's capital. With this money, the company intended to purchase "certain refining properties in Cleveland and elsewhere." By "certain refining properties", they meant every single refinery in Cleveland that did not already belong to Standard Oil.

Despite his meteoric rise in the world of business, John D. Rockefeller was not yet a familiar name in the newspapers. The brief, controversial existence of the South Improvement Company, or SIC, changed that forever. The South Improvement Company was a sort of holding company formed between Standard Oil, a couple of other smaller refineries, and the three major railroads: the New York Central, Erie, and Pennsylvania. Together, they made a pact, authorized by the Pennsylvania state legislature, whereby the railroads would double the going transport rates for all oil refineries with which it did business— but Standard Oil and its partner refineries would receive rebates of fifty per cent on those costs. Furthermore, the railroads would begin granting "drawbacks": for every barrel of oil the railroads transported from refineries outside the SIC, the

SIC refineries would receive *additional* rebates. In return for these rebates and drawbacks, Standard Oil agreed to patronize the three railroads at fixed percentages: the Pennsylvania Railroad was guaranteed to receive 45% of SIC business, while the Erie and New York Central railroads would receive 27.5% each. This kind of cooperation benefited the railroads just as much as it benefited the SIC, since they would no longer be in competition with each other for Standard Oil's business. The last contracts were signed, under conditions of absolute secrecy, in January of 1872.

It's unclear precisely how SIC intended to unveil this abrupt hike of shipping rates; even if things had gone according to plan, it's hard to imagine what kind of plan would have prevented a massive public outcry against it. Whether one admires Rockefeller or loathes him, there is little room to interpret the South Improvement Company scheme as anything but a secret conspiracy that was intended to ruin hundreds of small independent refineries. In any case, whatever the original public relations plan might have been, it was rendered useless after word of the rate hikes leaked out by accident. Railroad employees in strategic positions were informed of the rate hikes but told not to publish them until they were given further notice. One of these employees was called away from his post suddenly to visit his dying son; the man who took his place saw the list of new rates, and being unaware that they were supposed to remain secret, posted them that very day.

Word of the rate hikes spread like an oil fire and the result was nothing less than a popular uprising. One Cleveland refinery after another was swept into the Standard Oil fold—22 out of 26 belonged to Rockefeller's firm before the threat of the SIC dissipated—and the result was dubbed "the Cleveland Massacre". The name did not seem like an over-exaggeration at the time.

As one historian puts it: "For the horror-struck refiners in Titusville or Oil City, this wasn't simply a new competitive threat: It was a death warrant, and they stopped work and poured into the streets, denouncing the action in strident tones." People poured by the hundreds into town halls and opera houses to hear public speeches denouncing Rockefeller, whose name was now on everyone's lips. In one speech, Rockefeller was dubbed "the Monster" and his co-conspirators "the Forty Thieves". As it happens, Ida Tarbell was a girl of 14 living in Titusville when the public hue and cry against the South Improvement Company began; clearly, it made a distinct impression on the budding journalist.

Rockefeller was singularly unperturbed by the public fury sparked by the SIC fiasco. Despite the fact that he had gone from virtual obscurity to being tarred and feathered in the press virtually overnight, he was magnificently easy in his own conscience about the methods he had employed to seize supremacy over the oil industry. As far as he was concerned, there was nothing unethical about securing the rebates from the railroad companies—indeed, as he correctly pointed out, if the refineries of Oil Creek could have got them, they would have done the same as him. One might think that a man who prided himself on his strict Christian principles would be perturbed at the fact that many people now considered him to be grasping, greedy, and little better than a criminal, but Rockefeller had learned from an early age to turn a deaf ear to anything he considered idle talk. Indifference was a necessary defense mechanism when he was growing up, considering how much gossip his father's antics provoked. Furthermore, John and Cettie Rockefeller already kept their family as isolated from the wider world as possible. As strict Baptists, they believed that it was their destiny to be hated and misunderstand by a sinful world, because they had been entrusted with a mission—a divine calling of sorts. As Rockefeller explained to a reporter:

"I believe the power to make money is a gift from God—just as are the instincts for art, music, literature, the doctor's talent, the nurse's, yours—to be developed and used to the best of our ability for the good of mankind. Having been endowed with the gift I possess, I believe it is my duty to make money and still more money, and to use the money I make for the good of my fellow man according to the dictates of my conscience.""

In later years, many people were eager to claim that Standard Oil men, including Rockefeller himself, had threatened them in order to make them sell out. Rockefeller vehemently denied these claims; he never threatened, he only offered advice. But it is easy to see how the one might be mistaken for the other, since Rockefeller's version of advice was to warn the owner of a refinery that if he did not come into the Standard Oil fold, his business would go under within the year. To Rockefeller's mind, he was merely pointing out the obvious; small, independent refineries could not survive in the current state of the industry. Of course, those to whom he gave this advice held Rockefeller responsible for creating the conditions that made it impossible for small refineries to do business, so it was natural they felt menaced.

Nonetheless, Rockefeller was not devoid of ethics. He had certain principles to which he adhered strictly. When he bought a refinery, he tended to keep all of its staff, even the "deadwood", persons whose positions were technically redundant. Some refineries he purchased for more money than they were really worth, because he wasn't trying to destroy other people's livelihoods so much as he was trying to dictate the rate at which oil would sold to consumers. With other refineries, he made "running arrangements"—they remained independent, the property of their original owners, so long as they agreed to cap production at agreed upon levels. Yet at the same time, Rockefeller purchased some refineries for very small sums, only matching the price they would have fetched if they had been auctioned off for scrap. Philanthropy was important to Rockefeller, and sometimes philanthropy meant keeping on employees who were not strictly useful. But good business was good business, and sometimes business necessitated eliminating a refinery that was dragging the entire industry down. Rockefeller made the balance tally in the ledgers of his own conscience, and to him, that was all that really mattered.

The Pittsburgh Plan

The South Improvement Company soon had its charter revoked by the Pennsylvania state legislature—not because the company had violated any existing laws, but simply because some response was necessary to quiet the massive public outcry against it. A month later, however, the SIC had been replaced by the National Refiners' Association, popularly known as the Pittsburgh Plan. Where the SIC had been small and secret, a cabal composed of Standard Oil and the three major railroads, the Pittsburgh Plan was huge and public, uniting Standard Oil with the three biggest refiners in Pittsburgh: William G. Warden, William Frew, and O.T. Waring. Technically, all refineries were welcome to join the Pittsburgh magnates, but Rockefeller was so hated in the Oil Creek region that no one trusted his intentions. The National Refiner's Association, everyone believed, was just the South Improvement Company all over again.

One refinery owner after another came to Titusville, Pennsylvania, to discuss the terms of joining the Association. Rockefeller was present at some of these meetings, and one refiner left this impression of his manner and appearance during the negotiations:

"One day several of us met at the office of one of the refiners, who, I felt pretty sure, was being persuaded to go into the scheme which they were talking up. Everybody talked except Mr. Rockefeller. He sat in a rocking chair, softly swinging back and forth, his hands over his face. I got pretty excited when I saw how those South Improvement men were pulling the wool over our men's eyes, and making them believe we were all going to the dogs if there wasn't an immediate combination to put up the price of refined and prevent new people coming into the business, and I made a speech which, I guess, was pretty warlike. Well, right in the middle of it John Rockefeller stopped rocking and took down his hands and looked at me. You never saw such eyes. He took me all in, saw just how much fight he could expect from me, and I knew it, and then up went his hands and back and forth went his chair."

The Pittsburgh Plan lasted less than two months. This time, the problem wasn't the public outcry against it, but the tactics employed by people that Rockefeller referred to as "cheaters". The purpose of the Association, and the purpose of the SIC, had been to raise oil prices by reducing the amount of oil being refined for the market— hence the production caps that refineries were made to agree to. But some refineries joined the Pittsburgh Plan only to disregard those caps as soon as the price of oil went up again. Others allowed Rockefeller to buy them out, only to take the money, purchase better equipment, and open new refineries with better, more modern equipment. The lack of cooperation from these "cheaters" made Rockefeller dissolve the Association after only a month or so. His next attempt at engineering cooperation between refineries was the so called "Treaty of Titusville", in which he attempted to persuade refineries to pay double the going market rate for crude oil, and in return the producers who owned the oil wells would cap production at agreed upon levels. But the Treaty ran into the same problem as the Association; no one could stop individual refineries from breaking the terms of the agreement if they felt like it. It was becoming clear to Rockefeller that he could not achieve his goal of bringing the oil industry under strict regulation merely by forming confederations. Rockefeller needed to control not only the refiners but the producers themselves if the oil industry was going to adhere to his principles. And that meant that Rockefeller would have to go toe to toe with Oil Creek.

Lightning offensives

In 1873, the American economy, in a delayed reaction to the upheavals of the Civil War, suffered a crash and entered a six-year slump. Oil prices plummeted; in some parts of the country, oil was cheaper to transport than water. Rockefeller, the eternal optimist, saw the slump as an opportunity to create the monolithic oil empire of his dreams. Virtually all the refineries in Cleveland were now operating under the flag of Standard Oil; now Rockefeller set his sights on Pittsburgh and Philadelphia.

In the autumn of 1864, Rockefeller met privately with Charles Lockhart and William G. Warden, the heads of the largest refineries in Pittsburgh and Philadelphia, to extoll the benefits of joining Standard Oil. Rockefeller's secret weapon in these negotiations was to let the businessman he was wooing have a look at Standard Oil's books, the surest tangible proof of its profit margin. By this point, even in the midst of a depression, Standard Oil was doing so well that it could cut its prices to below the operating costs of the Pennsylvania firms and still make a profit.

Lockhart and Warden were suitably impressed, and practically overnight, Standard Oil had absorbed more than half the refineries in Pittsburgh and Philadelphia. Pretty soon, Rockefeller was acquiring the rest of the refineries in these cities and in New York, in what one historian refers to as "lightning offensives". As always, Rockefeller was careful to target the refineries that lay close to railroad hubs.

His next target was Oil Creek itself. Here, Rockefeller had a hard row to hoe. The oil came from Oil Creek, but Oil Creek was a poor location, financially speaking, for building and operating refineries, due to the cost of shipping chemicals and supplies into the rough terrain of the western Pennsylvania backwoods. But the people of western Pennsylvania were fiercely proprietary towards their refineries. Rockefeller explained the reason: the people of Oil Creek believed that "the place where the oil was produced, gave certain rights and privileges that persons seeking to engage in other localities had no right to presume to share." To Rockefeller's way of thinking, he was merely doing business; to the people of Oil Creek, he was usurping their God-given rights. So it came as a massive, demoralizing blow to the region when Rockefeller persuaded the owners of the Imperial Refining Company to sell to Standard Oil. Imperial was the principle refinery in the area, as much a symbol as a business, and when its owners capitulated to Rockefeller, the independent operators of Oil Creek considered them guilty of something like treason. But it was the beginning of the end of independent refining in the region; the second largest refinery in Oil Creek soon went over to Standard Oil, and the rest fell like dominoes. John D. Archbold, a 27-year old employee of the second refinery, had once given public speeches denouncing Rockefeller at opera houses and town halls. Now, Rockefeller brought him into the fold, and converted him into an ambassador. Archbold's job was to go among the independent refiners and persuade them to join Acme Oil Company— which was nothing more than a front for Standard Oil, but a front with a less poisonous name. Archbold was so successful in this and every other endeavor Rockefeller trusted him with that he quickly rose in the ranks of Standard Oil, as Rockefeller's hand-picked protégé.

Railroads

Rockefeller was well on his way towards controlling every major oil refinery in America, from Cleveland to Pittsburgh to West Virginia. He also had profitable, proprietary relationships with the three major railroads that served the oil region, which made it impossible for any independent refineries still holding out against Standard Oil to transport their product at less than exorbitant prices. There was, however, "one gaping hole left in the map: the territory controlled by the maverick Baltimore and Ohio (B&O) Railroad, whose tracks spanned southern Pennsylvania, connecting a cluster of refineries in Parkersburg and Wheeling, West Virginia, with an oil-export center in Baltimore.... In short, the B&O was providing comfort to the last independent refiners still holding out in open rebellion against his imperial rule."

Rockefeller navigated around this hold-out by secretly purchasing and renaming the largest refining center that the Baltimore and Ohio railroad serviced, J.N. Camden and Company. Camden, now the proprietor of the newly rechristened Camden Consolidated Oil Company, concealed his collaboration with Rockefeller from the railroad, and began to negotiate the same kind of shipping rebates for his refinery that Standard Oil was getting from the other three railroads. The president of the Baltimore and Ohio, of course, still believed that he was working against Standard Oil's interests. Camden proceeded to buy up all the other oil refineries in Baltimore, using his name and Standard Oil's money. By the time these purchases had been finalized in May of 1875, John D. Rockefeller had become "the sole master of American oil refining"—and as no major repositories of crude oil had yet been discovered anywhere else in the world, his dominance was not merely national, but global.

Now Rockefeller turned to the railroads themselves. In April of 1874, the Erie Railroad had given complete control of one of its New Jersey terminals to Standard Oil in exchange for fifty per cent of Standard Oil's business and help refitting its oil cars. A similar arrangement with the New York Central railroad followed shortly thereafter. Soon, the railroads were even more under the thumb of Standard Oil, as oil-tank train cars began to replace the old practice of piling oil barrels into freight cars. Presciently,

Rockefeller had begun purchasing the tank cars before the railroads did, so that practically all the tank cars in existence belonged to Standard Oil by the time the railroads were ready to adopt them. Since it was more profitable for the railroads to transport oil by tank car than by barrel, they were glad to lease the cars from Standard Oil in exchange for mileage rebates. Rockefeller used his strengthened bargaining position with the railroads to negotiate new terms that would spell the final doom of the Oil Creek refineries. The only advantage which the Oil Creek refineries had ever had over Cleveland was that the they were positioned closer to the oil wells, so their transport costs were lower, although Rockefeller had been eating away at that advantage for years. Now, Rockefeller demanded that the railroads institute uniform rates for all oil shipments—henceforth, oil being shipped from Cleveland would travel for the same price as oil being shipped from western Pennsylvania, despite the greater distance involved. If operating an independent refinery in

Oil Creek had been next to impossible before, it was now truly a fool's game.

The laying of the first successful pipelines briefly threatened Rockefeller's hegemony. Pipelines—underground pipes that tapped the subterranean oil reservoirs and allowed the oil to run like water through a spigot over immense land distances—had already made their first appearance when Rockefeller brought the railroads under his heel. But pipelines were a new technology, and the railroads, sensing the competition they would create, had been trying to delay their implementation. A successful pipeline network would make the railroads all but obsolete in the transportation of crude oil. Rockefeller, who usually championed emerging technologies, joined the railroads in halting technological progress in order to maintain a profitable status quo. But he quickly changed his tune when the Empire Transportation Company proved that the pipelines were essential to the future of the oil industry. Standard Oil quickly formed the American Transfer Company to lay its own pipeline structure, while Rockefeller purchased a one-third interest in the company that operated United Pipe Lines. As before, the last stronghold of resistance lay in Baltimore and West Virginia, where the Baltimore and Ohio Railroad remained independent. But by 1877, Standard Oil had purchased almost all the available refineries in Baltimore, leaving Rockefeller, at the age of 38, in control of 90% of all oil produced in the United States.

Tidewater

By 1879, Standard Oil was laying one and a half miles of new pipeline in the oil regions every day—a staggering pace, considering that the work was done by sheer manpower. Whenever a new oil well was struck, a representative from Standard Oil promptly appeared at the owner's front door, offering to connect his well to the pipeline. The owner's fortune was made for life, but as Standard Oil controlled all the pipelines in the region, and oil was now practically worthless unless it was connected to the pipeline, the owner was perennially dependent on Standard Oil and the rates it chose to pay. Woe betide the well owner who annoyed Rockefeller's agents in the area—if they refused to hook his well up to the pipeline, he would have no choice but to watch a fortune bubble up and trickle away.

The resentment against Standard Oil was still so strong in the Oil Regions that, notwithstanding the fact that any resistance could lead to the death of their livelihood, well owners in Titusville, Pennsylvania, formed a "Petroleum Parliament" to discuss plans for constructing two independent pipelines of their own which would lead east, to the sea. Up to this point, the longest pipeline covered only thirty miles overland. The Tidewater Pipeline Company was formed to run a pipeline from Oil Creek to Baltimore, but Standard Oil bribed members of the Maryland legislature to deny the company its charter. So the company instead began to build a pipeline that stretched 110 miles from Oil Creek to central Pennsylvania, laying down two miles of pipe per day. No one was certain whether the pipe would actually succeed in siphoning the oil, since the pipes had to travel up a mountainous incline of 2600 feet. Rockefeller himself was skeptical of Tidewater's ability to succeed in laying a working pipeline over such terrain, but he attempted to prevent it anyway. Standard Oil threatened to withdraw business from any of its suppliers that sold pipe to Tidewater; it purchased large tracts of valueless land in order to prevent pipeline construction in those areas; and when Tidewater compensated for this blocking maneuver by changing course and laying pipe over hilly terrain, Standard Oil agents circulated the countryside, warning farmers that the Tidewater pipeline was shoddily built and likely to leak oil into their land, ruining their crops.

When nothing else seemed capable of stopping the Tidewater pipeline, Standard Oil resorted to unprecedented amounts of outright government bribery to gain exclusive pipeline charters that would legally prevent any other pipelines being constructed in the state. During this era of American history, known as the Gilded Age because it saw the rise of so many of the first American millionaires, government bribery was considered a normal means of doing business, and did not carry the same legal or moral stigma it does today, which explains why Rockefeller did not find it objectionable on religious grounds. The bribes did not succeed in halting Tidewater's progress, however; advocates for free pipeline charters had brought their own bills before the legislature, and the best that Standard Oil's paid politicians could do was force those bills to a stalemate.

On May 28, 1879, construction on the Tidewater pipeline was completed. The pumps were activated at the pipe's point of origin in Bradford, Pennsylvania; seven days later, after scaling mountains and traveling over greater land distances than anyone thought possible, oil began to flow at the termination point in Williamsburg. Standard Oil was deeply dismayed, and Rockefeller's furious colleague, Daniel O'Day, who had organized the Standard Oil pipeline construction at Oil Creek, wanted to resort to outright physical sabotage to destroy the Tidewater line. But this, Rockefeller refused to allow. Instead, he reduced the rates charged by the Standard Oil pipelines, and the railroads reduced the rates for their oil-tank cars, until the prices fell so low that they were scarcely making a profit. For awhile, Tidewater was so stymied by this undercutting that it had to operate at half capacity. But then, Rockefeller got the surprise of his life: it turned out that Byron Benson, the man in charge of Tidewater, was, in one historian's words, "no more enamored of free markets than

Rockefeller was and had created the pipeline to join the feast." Benson communicated to Daniel O'Day that "he wanted to 'let the bar down', as he expressed it, for any overtures that might be made to his company, with a view of an adjustment of the pipe line questions. He said that he felt that the time had about come when the companies should work together with a view of preventing other companies from engaging in the business." No doubt this came as a nasty shock to the Oil Creek refineries who had looked to Tidewater as their source of liberation from Standard Oil. In 1882, Benson permitted Standard Oil representatives to buy a minority stake in Tidewater, and by the following year, the two companies had come to an agreement: Standard Oil would take 88.5 per cent of the pipeline business in Pennsylvania, and Tidewater would take the other 11.5 per cent. Rockefeller was again all-powerful in Oil Creek.

Chapter Six: Monopoly

"As Standard Oil secured complete control of the oil industry, many ordinary citizens were frightened by its gargantuan size, rapacious methods, and inexorable growth, and it came to symbolize all the disquieting forces reshaping America. It was the 'parent of the great monopolies which at present masquerade under the new-found name of "Trusts"', said one newspaper, and it served as shorthand for the new agglomerations of economic power. A business system based on individual enterprise was creating combinations of monstrous size that seemed to threaten that individualism. And modern industry not only menaced small-scale commerce but appeared to constitute a sinister despotism that endangered democracy itself as giant corporations overshadowed government as the most dynamic force in American society."

Ron Chernow, *Titan*

Ohio

There are a large number of respected scientists across the world who believe that we in the 21ˢᵗ century are living in the era of "peak oil"—in other words, that the oil fields of the earth are beginning to be depleted, necessitating a gradual shift to other, more sustainable forms of power. There are others who believe that the "cure" for peak oil was discovered in 2013, as methods such as hydraulic fracturing, or "fracking" began to be used to extract shale oil and natural gases from previously inaccessible bedrock. Whether or not American supplies of shale oil are as inexhaustible as some in the oil industry have claimed, most people today are unaware that in the late 1880s it was popularly believed that the era of peak oil had already arrived. At that point, western Pennsylvania still contained the world's only known deposit of crude oil, and it was considered only a matter of time before that deposit was depleted. In fact, the oil industry had been regarded as inherently unsustainable by Wall Street financiers since before John D. Rockefeller made his first investments in refineries. Many respectable bankers felt that extending loans to men like Rockefeller was tantamount to gambling. Eventually, the oil would dry up, speculators would go into bankruptcy, and the loans would never be recovered. Even after they witnessed the rise of the Standard Oil Trust and saw the massive amounts of money the oil industry was generating, many on Wall Street remained wary of a future without oil.

Behind closed doors, Rockefeller and his partners at Standard Oil were also worried. Together, they had supplied the world with vast amounts of kerosene and other petroleum byproducts, and in so doing had created a society that scarcely seemed capable of functioning without it. They too suspected that it was only a matter of time before the Pennsylvania oil fields were tapped dry. It was rumored that crude had been discovered in Russia, but that was scarcely helpful. Rockefeller had devoted decades of his life to organizing the American oil industry in such a way that he could dictate oil prices. Even if the Russian oil fields were bountiful, Rockefeller would undoubtedly have to pay dearly for Russian crude. Some of Rockefeller's partners were becoming so nervous about the future of the oil industry that they began floating the suggestion that Standard Oil should diversify into more stable commodities. Rockefeller alone retained his optimism about the industry's future.

Then, in 1885, oil was struck near Lima, Ohio. On a chemical level, it was inferior to Pennsylvania oil. Oil Creek crude had a paraffin base, and once it had been cleansed and treated with the sulfuric acid solution first discovered in the 1860s, it burned cleanly, without giving off films or odors. Ohio oil was different; even after being treated by sulfuric acid, it reeked of sulfur. Ohio oil had such an unpleasant smell, in fact, that it was nicknamed "skunk oil". No one was quite sure whether Ohio oil could ever be sold at the same price as Pennsylvania crude, and Rockefeller's partners at Standard Oil were dubious about its long-term prospects. Rockefeller, however, still possessed his unwavering belief that oil was the gift of a benevolent God to suffering mankind, and this gave him a positively supernatural faith in the longevity of the oil industry. He was determined that Standard Oil should make large investments in the Ohio oil fields. When his partners proved stubborn, Rockefeller made a bold proposal: he would make the investment in Lima out of his own money, to the tune of three million dollars. If the investment should prove successful, Standard Oil might reimburse him. If it proved otherwise, he would absorb the loss without a fuss. Rockefeller's partners were chastened by this announcement and decided to approve the company investment. Rockefeller had never led them wrong before, after all, and if he was bolder than other men, he was also considerably richer as a result of that boldness.

Rockefeller was a man of faith, but his was not a blind faith. Investing in the Ohio oil fields was a gamble, and he made sure to hedge this gamble from two directions. First, he hired a brilliant chemist named Herman Frasch, giving him a laboratory, money, and a single job: finding a way of treating the oil that would remove the foul odor. Next, he sent out teams of Standard Oil agents to businesses, hotels, railroads, factories, and warehouses, to pitch the idea of replacing coal for their furnaces with fuel oil. Kerosene, the leading product made from Pennsylvania crude, was ideal for lighting homes and shops and churches because it was bright and clean; but in industrial settings, the sulfurous smell of skunk oil wouldn't be so noticeable.

Like most of Rockefeller's gambles, this one paid off. Frasch found a means of eliminating most of the smell from the Ohio crude by using copper oxides to cleanse it of sulfur, although when burned in lamps the oil still left a slight film. The timing of this discovery was fortunate from a historical point of view; the Pennsylvania oil was indeed nearing depletion, and while the early 20th century would see the discoveries of huge oil deposits in Texas and Kansas, there was a gap of about a decade in which Ohio oil was the primary source for fossil fuels on earth. Also relevant from a historical point of view was the fact that Frasch was the world's first real petroleum chemist. In the 21st century, it is understood that industry and science go hand in hand, with industrial funding at the back of most major scientific research being conducted today, but in Rockefeller's time, the pairing of science and industry was a new innovation. It was a permanent one, however. By the time Rockefeller went into retirement, scientific laboratories had become a standard feature of every Standard Oil refinery.

Standard Oil promptly purchased three hundred thousand acres of land in Pennsylvania and West Virginia, and by 1891 it owned most of the Ohio-Indiana oil fields as well. The oil fields of Ohio stretched out for more than a hundred miles, and the terrain in the Midwest was not nearly so inaccessible as that of western Pennsylvania—for one thing, there were no mountain ranges between the oil and the major cities. Since there were no geographical obstacles to construction, and no point in shipping the oil from the Midwest to east coat refineries only to ship the refined oil products back to Ohio for sale, Standard Oil built a small refinery in Lima, and then a much larger state of the art refinery in Whiting, Indiana.

Unrivaled domination of the oil industry was what Rockefeller had been working towards practically his entire adult life, and now he had it. The Standard Oil Trust was comprised of many companies and had many shareholders, but in essence it was controlled by "a small clique of powerful families": the Pratts, the Payne-Whitneys, the Harness-Flaglers, and the Rockefellers, who owned a majority of the stock. These were Rockefeller's early business partners, in-laws, and other extended social and familial relations. For a nation that prided itself on its democratic values, it is easy to understand why the concentration of so much power, wealth, and influence in the hands of this small group of individuals made the public uneasy. Rockefeller himself was a principled man, even if those principles were not inconsistent, in his mind, with business practices that are today considered unethical. But the Standard Oil Trust was so huge and sprawling—it was dubbed the "Octopus", by political cartoonists in the newspapers of the day—that Rockefeller himself was forced to admit that sometimes unethical things were done by his representatives. He claimed that such situations were rectified promptly when brought to his attention, but this was not a satisfactory degree of oversight as far as the American public was concerned.

The Anti-Trust movement

The political power wielded by the Standard Oil Trust was immense, owing to the nature of Gilded Age graft. It was easy, if not inexpensive, to buy members of a state legislature, but the real path to influence lay in the fact that, prior to the passage of the 17th Amendment in 1912, senators were not elected by popular vote, but by their own state legislatures. It was thus possible for men and monopolies with deep pockets to send their approved candidates, not just to the state capital, but all the way to Washington D.C. By the late 1880s, the public was increasingly conscious of just how deeply enmeshed their elected officials were with massive trusts like Standard Oil, and a backlash ensued. "Muckraking" journalism, anti-trust coalitions, and Progressive activism were all born out of reaction to this deeply stewed environment of graft and mutual back-scratching.

There is no mention of trusts in the Constitution or the other foundational documents of American government, but American law had a great deal to say about the rights of property owners, so it took time to establish the legal precedents that would make it possible for Congress to restrict the size and scope of trusts and monopolies in American business. One such landmark case decided by the Supreme Court was *Munn v. Illinois,* in which a farmer's association brought a suit against a Chicago grain warehouse that was charging unfairly high prices for grain storage. The Court ruled in favor of the farmers, and found that:

"Whenever any person pursues a public calling, and sustains such relations to the public that the people must of necessity deal with him, and are under a moral duress to submit to his terms if he is unrestrained by law, then, in order to prevent extortion and an abuse of his position, the price he may charge for his services may be regulated by law."

The railroads were one of the chief targets of anti-trust activists, but this did not worry Rockefeller; thanks to pipelines, Standard Oil was far less dependent on the railroads than it had once been. More to the point, no one really expected that the railroads would abide by any government restrictions that were placed on it. Even if they did, Standard Oil could find a way to get around those restrictions. In 1887, the Interstate Commerce Act was passed, finally illegalizing the practice of railroad rebates and instituting the nation's first transportation regulatory commission—a necessity the founding fathers could scarcely have anticipated. Standard Oil made a dutiful public show of compliance with the new law, vowing that it would no longer accept rebates from the railroads, but in practice, the trust had already been skirting similar state-imposed regulations for a long time. Rockefeller's representative to the railroads, Colonel W.P. Thompson, explained to Rockefeller how this was being managed:

"Our arrangement is a very simple one: We are paying the open tariff rates to Michigan and all other points and this same is required of all other shippers. I have a distinct understanding with the proper persons that we are not required or expected to pay more than formerly and in order that we may not be out any money... we deduct from Chicago payments an equivalent amounting to what would have been a proper payment on all the other points, each month. You will readily see the object of this and you will observe in the situation we are in that no better or fairer arrangement could possibly have been made or one more satisfactory to us."

The fact of the matter was, Standard Oil still owned the massive fleet of oil-tank cars that the railroads used to do business with them, and therefore the railroads could not afford to alienate them—at least, not until the regulations were properly enforced, which would not begin to happen until the early 20th century.

Rockefeller before the New York senate

In 1888, when John D. Rockefeller was forty-eight years old, anti-trust fervor had reached such a pitch in the United States that both political parties were obliged to represent themselves as the enemy of trusts, despite the fact that many politicians were in the pockets of monopolies. The press had zeroed in on Rockefeller as the head of the Standard Oil hydra and were publishing constant editorials demanding that he be held accountable in some way. That year, a New York senate committee launched a formal inquiry into Standard Oil's business practices. Process servers were sent to Rockefeller's home and offices to present him with the summons that would require him to appear and give testimony, but they found Rockefeller a difficult man to track down—at least, until he was prepared to be found.

To prepare Rockefeller for his testimony, a lawyer was hired by Standard Oil and tasked with the job of drilling him on the responses he should give to the questions he might expect to have to answer during the hearing. But the lawyer, Joseph H. Choate, found Rockefeller frustratingly elusive; he could scarcely get a straight answer out of the old man on any matter pertaining to Standard Oil, even though Choate was technically on his side. Choate came away with the impression that Rockefeller was too absentminded too defend himself under cross-examination, but when he sounded this concern to Flagler, Rockefeller's business partner of many years, Flagler laughed. "Oh, you will find that he can take care of himself," Flagler assured Choate. "You needn't worry about him."

Flagler's insight was sound. When Rockefeller appeared in the hearing room to give testimony, it quickly became apparent to Choate that Rockefeller was a master showman, and that his show was all the more convincing for being anything other than showy. One historian describes how, "Under oath, [Rockefeller] turned into a vague and forgetful fellow, pleasant but slightly muddled, who wandered lost in the stupendous maze of Standard Oil." This performance worked considerably to Rockefeller's advantage, because Roger A. Pryor, the committee counsel who cross-examined him, was loud, querulous, and borderline abusive, strutting back and forth across the courtroom floor like a fire-and-brimstone preacher giving a sermon. Every major newspaper was present for the testimony and one reporter wrote that Rockefeller "[seemed] the embodiment of sweetness and light. His serenity could not be disturbed... In tones melodious, clear, and deliberate he gave his testimony... At times his manner was mildly reproachful, at others tenderly persuasive, but never did he betray an ill temper or vexation."

This was scarcely what the public had expected to find when they flocked to the courtroom to catch a glimpse of one of the richest and most powerful men in the world. But despite the mildness of Rockefeller's manners, his testimony caused a sensation. Not only was he obliged to tell the court facts about Standard Oil which had never been public knowledge before, such as the details of the 1882 trust agreement, the names of the current trustees, and the current number of shareholders, but for the first time in his career he was forced to comment publicly on the South Improvement Company, arguably the darkest blot on his name. However, the committee's lawyer made a crucial error: he asked Rockefeller whether he had ever been part of an organization called the *Southern* Improvement Company. As it happened, a charter had been granted for a company under that name; it had never been used, but technically, the company had existed. So it was with a clear conscience that Rockefeller was able to give the following testimony:

Pryor: "There was such a company?"

Rockefeller: "I have heard of such a company."

Pryor: "Were you not in it?"

Rockefeller: "I was not."

No perjury had been committed, but Rockefeller was undoubtedly abiding by the letter of the law and not the spirit. Yet even in his old age, Rockefeller felt neither guilt nor remorse over the incident, as he discussed it with William Inglis:

"I never undertake to instruct the man who asks me questions. I remember that incident as if it were this morning... I did not stop to correct my questioner. There is the record to stand on. Of course, I knew what I was answering... I did not testify like Mr. Brewster and Mr. Flagler, so hot-tempered that they would fly right into an argument with counsel. I was quiet and self-controlled. It was no part of my duty as a witness to volunteer testimony. While they thought they were leading me into a trap, I let them go into the trap themselves."

The New York senate committee hearing was far from the last time that Rockefeller would find himself in a courtroom answering for the actions of Standard Oil, but he was never found at a loss when giving testimony. One lawyer who examined him during later litigation, Samuel Untermyer, declared that Rockefeller was the canniest witness he had ever seen give testimony at a trial: "He could always read my mind and guess what the next six or seven questions were going to be. I would start with questions intended to lay the foundation for questions far in the future. But I would always see a peculiar light in his eyes which showed that he divined my intention. I have never known a witness who equaled him in this clairvoyant power."

It is probably fair to say that Rockefeller emerged from the 1888 hearing more personally popular than he had been before he gave testimony, but the same could not be said for Standard Oil's public image. The senate committee's findings were that Standard Oil was "the original trust" and that "Its success has been the incentive to the formation of all other trusts and combinations. It is the type of a system which has spread like a disease through the commercial system of this country." And Standard Oil was almost entirely Rockefeller's own brainchild; it was he who had figured out the best ways to suppress competition, rig markets, and take advantage of the free market. His career was essentially a road map for the anti-trust movement—all they had to do in order to draw up comprehensive trust-busting reform was look at what Rockefeller had done over the course of his career and outlaw those practices.

Nobody at Standard Oil took the anti-trust movement very seriously at first. Even after Rockefeller was hauled before the New York senate committee hearing, his partner, John Archbold, dismissed the possibility that any serious action would be taken in Washington.

The anti-trust movement was populist in nature, and Standard Oil had made its fortune by proving that a few educated men of business could thwart angry mobs numbering in the thousands, so long as they were properly organized against them. Anti-trust activists were just another mob in Archbold's eyes, like the Oil Creek independent refiners who had burned them in effigy. But this proved to be a miscalculation. A year and a half later, in 1889, an Ohio senator named John Sherman, brother of the famous Union general William T. Sherman, introduced the Sherman Antitrust Act, which was signed into law by President Benjamin Harrison in 1890. The Sherman Act "outlawed trusts and combinations in restraint of trade and subjected violators to fines of up to $5000, or a year's imprisonment or both."

However, the Act was so vaguely worded and so full of loopholes that for the next twenty years Standard Oil found that it posed little impediment to their carrying on business as usual. It was not until Ida Tarbell published *The History of Standard Oil Company* in 1904, inciting a fresh wave of furious anti-trust enthusiasm, that serious measures were taken to hold Standard Oil accountable by the terms of the Sherman Act. In 1909, the Department of Justice filed a federal anti-trust lawsuit against Standard Oil, citing the company's relationship with the railroads, its control of the pipelines, and its competition-cutting measures as grounds for its dissolution. This lawsuit, which went all the way to the Supreme Court, spelled the end of the company, which was ordered, in May of 1911, to dissolve into 34 separate companies, some of which survive to this day, including ExxonMobil and Chevron. But by then, Rockefeller had been retired for several years, and was devoting his energies to a completely different career. After spending the first fifty years of his life making money, he would spent the latter forty years figuring out new and inventive methods of giving it away.

Chapter Seven: Philanthropy

"Had John D. Rockefeller died in 1902, at the outset of the Tarbell series, he would be known today almost exclusively as a narrow man of swashbuckling brilliance in business, a man who personified the acquisitive spirit of late-nineteenth-century American industry. But just as the muckrakers were teaching the public that Rockefeller was the devil incarnate, he was turning increasingly to philanthropy. What makes him so problematic—and why he continues to inspire such ambivalent reactions—is that his good side was every bit as good as his bad side was bad. Seldom has history produced such a contradictory figure. We are almost forced to posit, in helpless confusion, at least two Rockefellers: the good, religious man, and the renegade businessman, driven by baser motives. Complicating this puzzle is the fact that Rockefeller experienced no sense of discontinuity as he passed from being the brains of Standard Oil to being the monarch of a charitable empire. He did not see himself in retirement as atoning for his sins, and he would have agreed emphatically with Winston Churchill's later judgement: 'The founder of the Standard Oil Company would not have felt the need of paying hush money to heaven.'"

Ron Chernow, Titan

Good works

Charitable giving had been a fixed aspect of Rockefeller's personal financial regimen since he was a boy in Moravia dropping pennies in the church collection plate under his mother's watchful eye. Long before he was wealthy, he had always found a few pennies or a few dollars to give to the needy. After he made his fortune, he began to receive a greater number of appeals, both from individuals and from charitable organizations, the latter often associated with the

Baptist church. Once he had more money to give, he made the giving of it into something of a personal hobby. Rockefeller had more leisure time built into his schedule than the astounding productivity of his career would suggest; he considered these private hours necessary to the preservation of his health, and since he often suffered crippling headaches, it is easy to understand why he tried to avoid exposing himself to too much stress. During these leisure hours, he sorted through the charitable requests he had received. Rather than delegating them to a secretary, he personally read all of the appeals, investigated the causes or the circumstances that had prompted the monetary request, wrote out the checks, and read the notes of gratitude he received in return. Rockefeller was more than willing to give money—he considered charitable giving to be the ultimate reason why God had permitted him to become rich—but he also believed he had a duty to see that the money he gave was put to the best use possible. He didn't grant every request that came his way and he never gave money without first making inquiries into the situation. People who asked for money without explaining why they needed it were turned away.

As Rockefeller grew more notorious, and thus, more famous, the number of charitable requests he received skyrocketed. There were mountains of letters to be sorted through daily. Worse, now that people knew just how much money he had, where he lived, and what he looked like, he was besieged by people asking for money on a daily basis, everywhere he went. New flocks of supplicants came looking for him every time a new article was published in the newspapers. Frederick T. Gates, a Baptist minister who would later head Rockefeller's philanthropic endeavors, remarked that Rockefeller was "constantly hunted, stalked, and hounded almost like a wild animal." It was one thing to be accosted in the street by a poor man begging for money to feed his family, or to receive a letter from a woman on the other side of the world claiming that God had told her to appeal to him. It was quite another when representatives from established charities invited themselves into his home, sometimes staying for days at a time. His leisure hours were dominated by these uninvited guests. As Rockefeller told William Inglis,

"The good people who wanted me to help them with their good work seemed to come in crowds. They brought their trunks and lived with me... At dinner they talked to me and, after dinner, when a little nap and a comfortable lounge or a restful chair and a quiet family chat seemed about the most desirable occupations until bedtime, these good people would pull up their chairs and begin, "Now, Mr. Rockefeller—." Then they would tell their story... There was only one of me and they were a crowd—a crowd increasing in numbers every day. I wanted to retain personal supervision of what little I did in the way of giving, but I also wanted to avoid a breakdown."

He did not, as it happens, succeed in avoiding that breakdown. In 1891, Rockefeller suffered a prolonged health crisis, the precise nature of which is somewhat uncertain. It is known that he suffered from digestive problems which could only be soothed by fasting on milk and crackers (although he was partial to milk and crackers and ate them even when he was in good health). He also fell prey to an influenza epidemic that was sweeping the nation, and at one point his doctor diagnosed him with both liver trouble and lung congestion. Rockefeller had always enjoyed excellent health up to that point, but now, in his mid-fifties, he was suffering the sudden effects of years of overwork. Strangely, it was not his work at Standard Oil that precipitated the crisis—it was his charity work, or rather, the combination of the two, because the charitable giving was becoming a full time job in itself. For a man like

Rockefeller, giving money away was immensely more difficult than making it, not because he was a tight-fisted old miser who hated to part with a single penny, but for precisely the opposite reason. The more money he made, the more money he wanted to give away; it was important to him that the scale of his giving matched the scale of his income. But because of his beliefs about the importance of good stewardship, he could not simply fling the money at anyone who wanted it. The necessity of doing good works conflicted with the impossibility of doing enough of them, and the crisis broke his health for a time.

Rockefeller eventually recovered from his illness after taking several months to rest and abstain from work of any kind. He moved to his family's country retreat and exercised, kept to a cautious diet, and gradually his strength and color began to return. By the time he was fit to return to work, it was beginning to dawn on him that there was no pressing reason for him to do so. After all, he had accomplished all that he had set out to do. He had organized the oil industry and made himself an extremely wealthy man. All that was left for him to do was to continue making money, and despite what people had been saying about him since he was a young man, making money had never been his life's goal. But he was only in his early fifties, too young to retire to a life of indolence and idleness. As luck would have it, the second of his full time jobs was waiting to absorb his energies. Rockefeller would spend the rest of his life making a science out of charitable giving, organizing philanthropy the way he had organized the oil industry.

University of Chicago

Rockefeller's first experiment in large-scale charitable giving arose out of his relationship with the Baptist church and his life-long interest in funding education. In 1881, at a church conference in Ohio, he had made the acquaintance of Harriet Giles and Sophia Packard, two teachers who had been educated at the Oread Institute, where Cettie Rockefeller had once studied. Giles and Packard were the founders of the Atlanta Baptist Female Seminary, a visionary institution that aimed to provide free black women in the south with an unrivaled liberal arts education. Rockefeller had been so impressed with the scope and planning that Giles and Packard had put into the project that he paid off all their debts. Afterwards, his wife Cettie, sister-in-law Lute, and their parents, the Spelmans, who had been fervent abolitionists before the war, continued to support the college. It was renamed Spelman Seminary in their honor, and today, Spelman College is one of the most renowned historically black colleges in the United States.

Rockefeller had continued to make donations to other educational institutions, especially favoring Baptist schools. Until the early 20th century, there was a dearth of prestigious colleges and universities in the United States compared to Europe, and all but a few of the best colleges were in the northeast. This was a problem for Baptists. Almost all institutions of higher learning had specific denominational affiliations, though by this point most of them admitted students of all religions. Harvard, Yale, and Dartmouth were Congregational (or Puritan), Columbia and the University of Pennsylvania were Episcopalian, and Princeton was Presbyterian; only Brown had Baptist antecedents. A Baptist minister named Augustus Strong, whose son Charles married the Rockefellers' oldest daughter, Bessie, spent years trying to persuade Rockefeller to build a magnificent new Baptist university in New York, with Strong serving as its president. The idea was not uninteresting to Rockefeller, but he disliked being dictated to, and Strong could scarcely restrain himself from badgering Rockefeller about it. He grew so strident that Rockefeller was finally forced to request, through an intermediary, that Strong not raise the subject with him ever again.

At the same time, the University of Chicago, founded thirty years earlier on a tract of land donated by famous Illinois politician Stephen A. Douglas, was on the verge of closing its doors due to financial mismanagement. As Chicago was a Baptist university, people began appealing for Rockefeller's help to salvage it; among these were Frederick T. Gates, who was then the executive secretary of the American Baptist Education Society. To Rockefeller, Gates pointed out the advantages of building a college in Chicago instead of New York—not only would land purchases and construction costs be cheaper in the Midwest, it was also the region of the country that contained the fastest-growing population of Baptists. The brightest and most talented of the children from these Baptist families would invariably be tempted east to Harvard or Yale, where they might fall under pernicious influences and shed the religion they were brought up with. If there was a first-rate university closer to home, however, it would undoubtedly attract young Baptists in droves.

Impressed by Gates' extensively researched report on the state of Baptist education in the United States, Rockefeller pledged a starting donation of $600,000 in the spring of 1889. Despite the size of this gift, and the many that would follow, Rockefeller would not allow his name to appear on any of the buildings on campus. (There is a Rockefeller Memorial on the university's campus today, but it was only so named after Rockefeller's death.) He was extremely keen to avoid any insinuations that his gifts to the college were made in an attempt to salvage his reputation in the eyes of those who considered him a robber baron. Likewise, he did not want the college to be associated with Standard Oil in any way, lest it be said that graduates were manufactured lackeys for the oil industry. He was so insistent that the college avoid any appearance of a connection with Standard Oil that an early version of the college seal was vetoed on the grounds that it featured a lighted lamp—a common Baptist symbol, but one that was apt to be misconstrued.

Rockefeller often had cause to complain of how his hand-picked university president, William Rainey Harper, was spending his donations. It was Harper's belief that all first-rate universities operated at a loss, a view which horrified Rockefeller, especially because it meant that Harper was continually running up debts which he expected Rockefeller to pay. But no one could deny that Harper was putting the money to good use. When the school opened its doors for the first time in October of 1892, it was already considered one of the finest universities in the world, owing to the fact that Harper had used Rockefeller's money to poach the best teachers and most renowned academics in the scholastic world for his faculty. There were 750 students enrolled on the first day of classes. A quarter of them were women; ten were Jewish, eight were Catholic, and a small number were black. For the American Midwest in 1892, this qualified as extraordinary diversity. Only Oberlin College in Ohio, which had been admitting black students and women since before the Civil War, was more liberal in its admissions policies.

Organized giving

When speaking of his work with the University of Chicago, Rockefeller explained the thinking that eventually guided him to pouring millions of dollars into organized charitable agencies:

"Following the principle of trying to abolish evils by destroying them at the source, we felt that to aid colleges and universities, whose graduates would spread their culture far and wide, was the surest way to fight ignorance and promote the growth of useful knowledge. That has been our guiding principle, to benefit as many people as possible. Instead of giving alms to beggars, if anything can be done to remove the causes which lead to the existence of beggars, then something deeper and broader and more worthwhile will have been accomplished."

Needless to say, Rockefeller had no patience for any school of thought which suggested that monopolies like Standard Oil was one of those entities which causes "beggars" to be created, nor could he ever have been brought around to that way of thinking. He was fixed in his principles; the Protestant work ethic ran deep in his blood. But this desire to get at the root causes of social problems, combined with his unique genius for organizing large scale endeavors, led to the creation of our modern system of targeted philanthropy and non-profit charitable institutions.

In 1891, while his health was still in a precarious state, Rockefeller turned to Frederick Gates with a proposal:

> "I am in trouble, Mr. Gates," [said Rockefeller]. "The pressure of these appeals for gifts has become too great for endurance. I haven't the time or strength, with all my heavy business responsibilities, to deal with these demands properly. I am so constituted as to be unable to give away money with any satisfaction until I have made the most careful inquiry into the worthiness of the cause. These investigations are now taking more of my time and energy than the Standard Oil itself. Either I must shift part of

the burden, or stop giving entirely. And I cannot do the latter."

"Indeed you cannot, Mr. Rockefeller," Gates replied.

"Well, I must have a helper. I have been watching you. I think you are the man. I want you to come to New York and open an office here. You can aid me in my benefactions by taking interviews and inquiries and reporting the results for action. What do you say?"

Gates said yes, and promptly moved his family to New York to start work. As executive secretary of the American Baptist Educational Society, he already had an infrastructure of contacts and causes to begin working with, and during his first year of work he used Rockefeller's money all over the country to fund various charitable causes. By 1892, Gates was in a position to inform Rockefeller that "Our denomination has a larger, better distributed, better organized, and more efficient education property than any other denomination in America."

Gates had an excellent mind for public relations; by steering Rockefeller's money to his own handpicked causes, he managed to avoid what Rockefeller most wanted to avoid, which was the appearance that his charitable giving was driven by ulterior motives, either to somehow further Standard Oil's interests or to "cleanse" his reputation. Rockefeller initially inclined towards charities that supported his political interests, such as the temperance movement. Gates, however, gently moved him towards supporting "programs with broad appeal and universal support—things unarguably good that helped all classes of people and lacked any tincture of self-interest." Rockefeller states in his memoirs that his charities targeted six broad categories of relief: "(1) material comforts (2) government and law (3) language and literature (4) science and philosophy (5) art and refinement (6) morality and religion." No one could argue with goals such as these.

One of Rockefeller's most perplexing dilemmas was how to give money to people without lessening their self-reliance. Another passage from his memoirs provides a comprehensive statement of his belief system, steeped in the Protestant work ethic and the conservative belief that self-respect derives from labor:

"I believe in the supreme worth of the individual and in his right to life, liberty and the pursuit of happiness.

I believe that every right implies a responsibility; every opportunity, an obligation; every possession, a duty.

I believe that the law was made for man and not man for the law; that government is the servant of the people and not their master.

I believe in the dignity of labor, whether with head or hand; that the world owes no man a living but that it owes every man an opportunity to make a living.

I believe that thrift is essential to well-ordered living and that economy is a prime requisite of a sound financial structure, whether in government, business or personal affairs.

I believe that truth and justice are fundamental to an enduring social order.

I believe in the sacredness of a promise, that a man's word should be as good as his bond, that character—not wealth or power or position—is of supreme worth.

I believe that the rendering of useful service is the common duty of mankind and that only in the purifying fire of sacrifice is the dross of selfishness consumed and the greatness of the human soul set free.

I believe in an all-wise and all-loving God, named by whatever name, and that the individual's highest fulfillment, greatest happiness and widest usefulness are to be found in living in harmony with His will.

I believe that love is the greatest thing in the world; that it alone can overcome hate; that right can and will triumph over might."

The key to his philanthropic dilemma rests in this statement: "that the world owes no man a living but that it owes every man an opportunity to make a living." Advocates of social welfare, universal healthcare, supplemental nutritional assistance programs, low-income housing, and other such staple causes of progressive politics, might take serious issue with the notion that no human being is "owed a living". Most people do not prefer to be idle all their days, but there are many circumstances under which people are not capable of "earning a living" in a capitalist system. In Rockefeller's day, however, these were comparatively new ideas, and they would not have appealed to him in any case. He was capable of recognizing the damaging effects of cyclical poverty, but not of divining its true sources. As one biographer puts it, "He dreaded the thought of armies of beggars addicted to his handouts." Furthermore, he genuinely believed that the social order existed for a reason, that the poor were only poor because they were in some way inferior—less intelligent, less hard working—than the rich. He believed that "the failures that a man makes in his life are due almost always to some defect in his personality, some weakness of body, mind or character, will or temperament... It is my personal belief that the principal cause for the economic differences between people is their difference in personality, and that it is only as we can assist in the wider distribution of those qualities that go to make up a strong personality that we can assist in the wider distribution of wealth."

In short, Rockefeller believed that his money would be put to best use in shaping people's "personalities" so that they were better suited to making money for themselves. Rockefeller opened no soup kitchens, and awarded pensions only in individual cases. Prevention, rather relief, was his goal, and the road to prevention was to be paved by science.

Medical research

Rockefeller was strongly influenced by the philanthropic endeavors of his fellow millionaires; Andre Carnegie had written essays that put forth the idea that rich men ought to give their money away rather than leave it to be squandered by potentially worthless heirs. Johns Hopkins had devoted his railway fortune to establishing Johns Hopkins University in Baltimore, one of the finest universities in the world. Medical research held a special, almost nostalgic appeal for Rockefeller, who remembered the "physic bush" his grandmother had used to concoct general-purpose remedies when he was a boy; at one point, he had cuttings from that bush sent to one of his medical research laboratories to find out whether it did, in fact, have any healing properties. Though schools of medicine existed in abundance, they were often mere diploma mills; the concept of a medical research institution had scarcely been dreamt of in the United States until Rockefeller's time. Frederick Gates, after doing extensive research into the present state of medical research and education, discovered that while the existence of diseases and their symptoms had been well documented by generations of doctors, there had been scarcely any formal inquiry into the root causes of disease, for instance, on the microbial level. As it happened, the science of bacteriology was just beginning to flourish, and "specific microorganisms were being isolated as the causes of disease". Inspired by these discoveries, Gates turned to Rockefeller with an impassioned proposal: a medical research institute along the lines of the Pasteur Institute, founded in Paris in 1888, and the Koch Institute for Infectious Diseases, founded in Berlin in 1891. Characteristically plodding when it came to making a major decision, Rockefeller let the idea simmer for two years before he gave Gates the approval for the project.

The American medical community at the time was divided between two schools of thought; allopaths, who believed that cures for disease lay in inducing symptoms that were different from the symptoms of a disease (such as administering aspirin to reduce a fever) and homeopathy, which attempted to cure diseases by inducing symptoms similar to the disease in lesser quantities. Gates dismissed both schools of medical thought as useless, harmful, and unscientific. It might justifiably be said that it was Frederick Gates who was responsible for creating an emphasis on research-based medicine in the United States, because it was he who supervised the endowment of the Rockefeller Institute for Medical Research in New York, the first research facility of its kind in America. Doctors and researchers would be hired, funded, and given laboratory space; from there, it was up to them to mark out their own lines of research and find out what they could.

This was later considered to be the secret of the RIMR's success: scientists, not accountants, were placed in charge of expenditures. The RIMR was to "Gather great minds, liberate them from petty cares, and let them chase intellectual chimeras without pressure or meddling. If the founders created an atmosphere conducive to creativity, things would, presumably, happen."

The medical research funded by Rockefeller probably gave him greater personal satisfaction than any other single charitable endeavor he undertook. Gates once wrote that,

"I make it my business to keep Mr. Rockefeller personally informed of every important thing done and every promising line of inquiry at the Institute. He knows the lines of experiment trembling on the verge of success and their thrilling promise for humanity. I have seen the tears of joy course down his cheeks as he contemplated the past achievement and future possibilities of the Institute. He is a man of very quick and tender sympathies just as he is a man of a keen and lively sense of humor."

The first major result of the RIMR's research was the Flexner serum. In the winter of 1904-1905, a cerebrospinal meningitis epidemic broke out in New York, killing three thousand people. Flexner, the brilliant doctor Rockefeller had personally recruited to head the facility, immediately set to work on a treatment, and after concocting a serum which proved to cure the disease in monkeys, the RIMR opened its doors to the public, administering the cure for free to all afflicted persons who presented themselves for help. Though meningitis is now treated with antibiotics and sulfa drugs, Flexner's serum nonetheless saved hundreds of lives. Suddenly, Rockefeller was famous for something other than running an oil monopoly. He promptly bestowed another 2.6 million dollars on the institute. Five years later, the RIMR opened its first adjoining hospital, boasting a ward with sixty beds, as well as a nine bed isolation unit. The hospital treated for free any person afflicted with one of the five diseases then being prioritized for research: polio, pneumonia, syphilis, heart disease, and intestinal infantilism (now known as celiac disease).

When Rockefeller was near death, Winston Churchill wrote:

"When history passes its final verdict on John D. Rockefeller, it may well be that his endowment of research will be recognized as a milestone in the progress of the race. For the first time, science was given its head; longer term experiment on a large scale has been made practicable, and those who undertake it are freed from the shadow of financial disaster. Science today owes as much to the rich men of generosity and discernment as the art of the Renaissance owes to the patronage of Popes and Princes. Of these rich men, John D. Rockefeller is the supreme type."

John D. Rockefeller's last years

Rockefeller's wife, Cettie, had started to decline in health in 1909; she was so weak that she was confined to a wheelchair, which had to be carried up the front steps of her New York residence, and she spent most of her time in bed. Despite the fact that the finest medical minds in America worked for her husband, she was strangely reluctant to consult them, even though she suffered from pneumonia, shingles, pernicious anemia, and sciatica. Throughout her long final period of illness, Rockefeller switched back and forth between the roles of the loving, devoted husband he had been all throughout their marriage, and the boy who had always dreaded witnessing suffering and death. When they were together, he was unfailingly attentive to Cettie, even romantic; but he spent more time away from her than one would expect of a devoted husband. By this point in his life, he stuck to a strict seasonal schedule, rotating between houses in four different states; officially, he was a resident of the state of New York, and paid his income taxes there, but there was a danger that if he lingered past a certain date at any of the houses he kept in other states, they would also claim him as a resident in an effort to get tax money out of him. The need to keep to this schedule kept him from Cettie's side for weeks at a time, but she never seemed to resent his absences.

In 1913, Cettie added lumbago, pleurisy, and congestive heart failure to her list of medical complaints. Her condition deteriorated to such a degree that her doctors informed Rockefeller that she could not be moved from her house in Cleveland. At that point, Rockefeller braved the threat of the tax collectors and stayed close to Cettie, taking her for drives in carriages and in his favorite car—the invention of the automobile had delighted him, and he owned several, racing them as he had once raced horses. Cettie and John attended Euclid Avenue Baptist Church when they could, the congregation they had attended for many years when their family was young, and one one occasion Rockefeller was asked to address the congregation. His eyes fell on his wife, sitting in the pew, and he paused his remarks to say that, "People tell me I have done much in my life. I know I have worked hard. But the best thing I ever accomplished, and the thing that has given me the greatest happiness was to win Cettie Spelman. I have had but one sweetheart and am thankful to say I still have her."

In February of 1914, Rockefeller had one of the family's New York residences remodeled so that Cettie could get around more easily, but Cettie was reluctant to leave the Euclid Avenue house where her children had grown up. "Mr. John's little rocking chair is upon the attic floor," she murmured softly to her nurse. In September of that year, the Rockefellers celebrated their 50th wedding anniversary, and Rockefeller arranged for a brass band to play Mendelssohn's "Wedding March" on the front lawn while Cettie was carried, bridal style, from the house. Cettie's spirits improved a great deal during the last months of her life; she declared that she felt stronger and began to spend more time outdoors. Nonetheless, in the early spring of 1915, Cettie Spelman Rockefeller lay down for a nap after taking a turn in the garden and drinking a glass of milk. She quickly lapsed into unconsciousness, and at 10 the next morning she breathed her last. Her doctor and her sister Lute were sitting by her bedside as she died.

Rockefeller was at his home in Ormond Beach, Florida, when the news of Cettie's death reached him. Two telegrams arrived one after the other, the first announcing that Cettie was near death, and the second that she had died. Despite her long illness, the news hit Rockefeller with all the force of a sudden shock. His son, John Jr., and daughter-in-law Abby were sitting at the breakfast table when Rockefeller came to tell them the news. Junior would remark later that it was the first time in his life he had ever seen his father cry. Years later, Rockefeller would tell his daughter Edith, who had been out of the country when her mother died, that Cettie had "triumphed gloriously when the end came, and to the last view we took of her, her face bore that angelic radiance." Mementoes of their early married life became especially precious to him, such as the first set of dishes they had bought as a couple to adorn their dinner table.

True to Rockefeller's worries, the Cleveland tax office seized on the extra months he had spent with Cettie in Cleveland as an excuse to demand taxes from him. Rockefeller had long felt that the city of Cleveland treated him with a special kind of unwarranted vindictiveness, despite all he had done for its economy, and the many generous public gifts he had made to the city—donations to churches, universities, and the orchestra, plus land for two public parks. Now, his dispute with the tax collectors prevented him from burying Cettie at the family plot which had long been prepared for her in Cleveland. For a short time, Cettie was interred in the family mausoleum belonging to their old friend, John Archbold.

In order to get Cettie buried in Cleveland, Rockefeller had to resort to subterfuge. The Archbold mausoleum was under guard, lest Cettie's remains be disturbed. (The Rockefeller name was so legendary at this point that in 1930, one woman tried to buy the ramshackle cottage in Richmond, New York, where Rockefeller had been born, so that she could have it transferred to the city and charge admission to tourists who were curious to see evidence of the famous millionaire's humble antecedents; it was therefore not unthinkable that someone might try to remove Cettie's body or claim some strange souvenir from it.) One night, during a rainstorm, the guards were called away under a false pretext, and a local undertaker loaded Cettie's casket into a plain unmarked box in the back of his hearse. He then put the disguised casket onto a train bound for Cleveland; the railroad employees knew that he was transporting a corpse, but not its identity. Rockefeller, his daughter Alta, her husband Parmalee, and Cettie's sister Lute were waiting at the Cleveland cemetery when Cettie's remains arrived. She was interred in one of three plots arranged in a row—Eliza, Rockefeller's mother, was buried on one side, Cettie was buried on the other, and the final, empty plot was reserved for Rockefeller, "so that [he] could spend eternity flanked by his two favorite women." When the service was over, the family departed quietly. Rockefeller never returned to Cleveland.

John D. Rockefeller would live for another twelve years. By the time of Cettie's death in 1915 he had already given over the management of all his philanthropic agencies to his capable staff; the last gift he personally endowed was the Laura Spelman Rockefeller Memorial, which for years championed research into the social sciences. He had long since handed over control of the family business to John Jr., and given him the bulk of his money, with settlements made on his other children as well. When John's son Laurance was born in 1910, they explained that they had chosen to spell his name this way in honor of his grandmother, Cettie, whose real first name was Laura. Laurance was said to be the grandchild who looked and acted the most like "Senior", as Rockefeller was known to his family by then.

As Rockefeller grew older, he naturally saw less of his children and grandchildren and great-grandchildren. His relationship with his daughter Edith was troubled; she had traveled to Europe in 1913 to seek treatment for depression and ended up studying with Carl Jung, under whose tutelage she learned to probe the depths of her own feelings and memories. Understandably, this produced a host of confused feelings towards her father, who had been gentle and loving yet strangely aloof and guarded, a resolute and reticent Victorian who baffled his free-thinking daughter. Rockefeller and Edith wrote to one another regularly, and their correspondence betrays both the love and the frustration they felt towards one another. Though Edith returned to America in 1921, she did not visit her father. In 1932, after suffering a bout of breast cancer and a mastectomy, she died at the age of sixty; Rockefeller had not seen her for twenty years.

Rockefeller spent much of his time in Ormond Beach, Florida, where he had built an estate called The Casements. During the 1920s, his favorite hobbies were gold and playing the stock market—a pastime which often necessitated that he "borrow" back some of the money he had bestowed on his son John. "John," he would say, "I've been following the stock market carefully. I think that if I had a little money, I could use it to make some more. Do you believe you could lend me several hundred thousand dollars?" To which John Jr. would reply, "Well, father, do you think you are old enough to use it wisely?" After the stock market crash of 1929, the fortunes of both father and son were slashed dramatically; from a stockpile of twenty-five million dollars, John Rockefeller was reduced to seven million, while John Jr. was reduced from one billion dollars to five hundred million. No one in the Rockefeller family was going to go hungry during the Depression, to be sure, but it was less money than Senior had had at his disposal since he was a much younger man, and it made him quite nervous.

When Rockefeller reached his tenth decade on earth, he underwent a curious change of personality. Many elderly people lose some of their edge, and grow irritable under the resulting mental confusion; Rockefeller, by contrast, seemed to expand in happiness and good cheer. The lifelong reserve he had clung to like a shield seemed to melt away, and a sort of open-heartedness replaced it. He had shrunk to less than a hundred pounds, but he was still an avid golfer up until 1932, when a severe cold forced him to cut down on the number of rounds he played each day, until at last he abandoned the sport altogether. Yet a newspaper reporter who came to see him the year he turned 93 reported that, "He was so delighted to be out in the warm sunshine again that once he stopped and sang a hymn as he gazed with twinkling eyes at the myriad of brilliant flowers and shrubs." His dearest wish was to live to see the age of 100.

Ever a man to disdain ostentatious displays of wealth and luxury, he grew even more contemptuous of them near the end of his life. George Rigby, a personal friend and the mayor of Ormond Beach, recalled that one day they were looking out over the water when Rockefeller spotted a yacht in the distance. His reaction brings to mind the confrontation he once had with George Gardner in Cleveland, who had disgusted him by buying a share in a yacht:

"I recall one day we were sitting on his front porch at Ormond watching a most elaborate yacht winding its way down the Halifax River toward Palm Beach. [Rockefeller] expressed his wonder at the possible pleasure a man could get out of such show and pretension. Then, after a moment or two, the whole expression of his face changed and he asked enthusiastically, 'Wasn't that a beautiful rain we had last night?'"

In 1934, when Rockefeller was 95, he contracted pneumonia. Though he recovered, he was considerably weakened, and he decided to spend the rest of his days in Great Ormond, conserving his energy so he could "eke out five more years". His mind remained sharp, but he no longer went on garden walks or took long car rides. He spent most of his days sitting on the front porch with a blanket over his legs, soaking in the sun, though he took a little exercise every day by riding on a stationary exercise bike. He enjoyed a last financial triumph when he turned 96 years old; the life insurance company which had carried his policy for years was obliged to pay him the sum of five million dollars. Only one man in 100,000 born the year that Rockefeller was born lived to see that age.

Rockefeller was extremely fond of movies, and though he was often too weak to attend church, he would turn on the radio on Sunday mornings to listen to a broadcast of a sermon. One day, when automobile titan Henry Ford was leaving after a visit, Rockefeller remarked, "Good bye, I'll see you in heaven," to which Ford jokingly replied, "You will if you get in." But Rockefeller entertained no doubts on that score. When he was 86, he had written a short poem that seemed to summarize his feelings about his life with greater poignancy than his memoirs or any of his longer prose works:

I was early taught to work as well as play,

My life has been one long, happy holiday;

Full of work and full of play—

I dropped the worry on the way—

And God was good to me everyday.

For a man who sees his life in such terms, it might be argued that heaven has already been attained.

Like his wife Cettie, John Rockefeller seemed to grow stronger in the last few months before his death than he had been for a long time. The day before he died, he was sitting out in the sun with Fanny Evans, a cousin of his who was thirty years his junior, and who had come to live with him as his housekeeper after Cettie died. "Mr. Rockefeller," she told him, "the sun has given you some color. You look so much better." When he only smiled and bowed without returning the compliment, she chided him for his lack of chivalry: "Mr. Rockefeller, you haven't said anything about how I look." Rockefeller replied, "Mrs. Evans, that is because I am never able to do the subject justice." Later that evening, as if struck by some premonition of his impending mortality, he made one final charitable gesture, and paid the mortgage on the Euclid Street

Baptist Church in Cleveland. By the end of the day, he had suffered a heart attack; at 4 in the morning, on May 23, 1937, John D. Rockefeller breathed his last. He was just two months shy of his 98th birthday.

Other great books by Michael W. Simmons on Kindle, paperback and audio:

Elizabeth I: Legendary Queen Of England

Alexander Hamilton: First Architect Of The American Government

William Shakespeare: An Intimate Look Into The Life Of The Most Brilliant Writer In The History Of The English Language

Thomas Edison: American Inventor

Catherine the Great: Last Empress of Russia

Romanov: The Last Tsarist Dynasty

Peter the Great: Autocrat and Reformer

The Rothschilds: The Dynasty and the Legacy

Queen Victoria: Icon of an Era

Six Wives: The Women Who Married, Lived, and
Died for Henry VIII

Further Reading

Titan: A Life of John D. Rockefeller, Sr., by Ron Chernow

The History of Standard Oil Company, by Ida Tarbell

> https://ia800208.us.archive.org/27/item
> s/historyofstandar00tarbuoft/historyofst
> andar00tarbuoft_djvu.txt

Random Reminiscences of Men and Events, by John D. Rockefeller

.

Made in the USA
Monee, IL
12 December 2020